D0116803

Marriage

AMERICAN IDEALS AND INSTITUTIONS SERIES

Robert P. George, series editor

Published in partnership with the James Madison Program in American Ideals and Institutions at Princeton University, this series is dedicated to the exploration of enduring questions of political thought and constitutional law; to the promotion of the canon of the Western intellectual tradition as it nourishes and informs contemporary politics; and to the application of foundational Western principles to modern social problems.

Marriage

The Dream That Refuses to Die

Elizabeth Fox-Genovese

edited by Sheila O'Connor-Ambrose

Wilmington, Delaware

Fox-Genovese, Elizabeth, 1941–2007.

Marriage : the dream that refuses to die / Elizabeth Fox-Genovese ; edited by Sheila O'Connor-Ambrose.—1st ed.—Wilmington, Del. : ISI Books, c2008.

p. ; cm.
(American ideals & institutions)

ISBN: 978-1-933859-62-0
Based on three lectures delivered at Princeton University in December 2003.
Includes index.

1. Marriage—United States. 2. Family—United States. 3. Marriage—United States—Religious aspects—Christianity. 4. Same-sex marriage—United States—Religious aspects—Christianity. 5. Family—United States—Religious aspects—Christianity. I. O'Connor-Ambrose, Sheila. II. Title. III. Series.

HQ536 .F69 2008   2008921547
306.8/0973—dc22   0805

ISI Books
Intercollegiate Studies Institute
Post Office Box 4431
Wilmington, DE 19807-0431
www.isibooks.org

Book design by Beer Editorial and Design
Manufactured in the United States of America

Contents

Editor's Acknowledgments

I am deeply grateful to my family for helping me to finish this piece of Betsey's work. They loved Betsey dearly and continue to believe in the importance of her vision and work. My parents, Charles and Mary Alice O'Connor, read everything, and Betsey herself sought out the comments of my sister and brother-in-law, Molly and Edward O'Connor, on these lectures and other of her writings. Douglas Ambrose, who understands Betsey's work far better than I, makes everything possible and even joyful. And my children, Antonia, Augusta, and Dominic, who love and miss their "Aunt Bessie," found my attempts to work in their noisy midst both bothersome and amusing, which is as it should be.

I am grateful as well to Robert P. George, who entrusted me with this work, and to Jeremy Beer for his steadfast confidence and good cheer. I am indebted to Tina Trent, Betsey's second-to-last student and true friend, for her insightful comments, invaluable suggestions for additional essays, and, most important, her sterling heart. And heartfelt thanks to Rebecca Fox, not only for answering my biographical question about Betsey, but for her kindness and empathy, which made all the difference.

Many years ago, when I was finishing my doctoral exams, Betsey predicted that one day I would "write an essay about one of Gene's beloved Southern ladies and dedicate it to him." She had in mind, of course, the likes of Augusta Jane Evans or Louisa McCord. But as I was finishing this project, the memory of that long-forgotten conversation floated into my consciousness. So I dedicate my work, as paltry as it is, to Gene, and I know in my heart the consolation of a promise kept to his beloved lady, Betsey.

Editor's Note

Part One of *Marriage: The Dream That Refuses to Die* began as a series of lectures Elizabeth Fox-Genovese delivered at Princeton University in December 2003. Part Two consists of selected previously published essays and lectures on history, family, and women's lives. We are grateful for permission to republish these works, whose copyrights remain with their respective owners.

"Women and the Family" originally appeared in *Women and the Future of the Family*, with responses by Stanley J. Grenz, Mardi Keyes, and Mary Stewart Van Leeuwen, edited by James W. Skillen & Michelle V. Noll (Grand Rapids, MI: Baker Books, 2000). "Thoughts on the History of the Family" appeared in *The Family*,

Civil Society, and the State, edited by Christopher Wolfe (Lanham, MD: Rowman & Littlefield, 1998). "The Legal Status of Families as Institutions" was first published in *Cornell Law Review* 77 (1992): 992–96. "Historical Perspectives on the Human Person" was originally published in the *Fellowship of Catholic Scholars Quarterly* 24, no. 2 (Spring 2001): 2–7. "The Family and John Paul II" first appeared as "John Paul II on the Family" in *John Paul II—Witness to Truth,* edited by Kenneth D. Whitehead (South Bend, IN: St. Augustine Press, 2001), 12–24, and was reprinted in *Columbia Magazine,* September 2003. Robert P. George's afterword was first published as "The Story of a Well-Lived Life: Elizabeth Fox-Genovese, R.I.P.," *National Review Online,* January 3, 2007.

For the sake of clarity, it should be pointed out that the list of "good books on marriage" which begins on page 171 was compiled by the editor, not the author.

Introduction

Sheila O'Connor-Ambrose

M *arriage: The Dream That Refuses to Die* did not begin as a book, but rather as a series of three lectures delivered at Princeton University in late 2003 by Elizabeth Fox-Genovese, the Eléonore Raoul Professor of the Humanities and founding director of the Department of Women's Studies at Emory University. Betsey—her father loved to call her "Betsey Ann"—was invited to Princeton by Robert P. George (the school's McCormick Professor of Jurisprudence and director of the James Madison Program in American Ideals and Institutions) to be the Madison Program's Charles E. Test, M.D., Distinguished Visiting Scholar in 2003–4. This invitation pleased and honored Betsey deeply, for, as Professor George noted in his letter, only someone who "exemplifies the highest possible standards of excellence in the humanities and social sciences" is asked to be the Test Scholar.

The lectures would be substantial—three of them, each ninety minutes in length, including a question-and-answer period—and Betsey decided to focus them on the historical, moral, and cultural foundations of marriage, a hotly contested topic that was swiftly becoming a major national debate even before the Massachusetts Supreme Judicial Court's decision on November 18, 2003, that redefined marriage in the commonwealth by eliminating sexual complementarity as an element of marriage. The lectures, which Betsey delivered in sequence on December 1, 3, and 8, 2003, were compelling, subtle, and carefully reasoned. They were historically grounded in a sure-footed consideration of epochs from pre-Christian cultures to nineteenth-century Cherokee traditions to present-day Massachusetts; they were fully engaged in complex contemporary discussions; and they were sprinkled with valuable literary, theological, legal, and sociological insights.[1]

Professor George and others—recognizing the lectures as a gift to those who care deeply about marriage—urged Betsey to publish them as a book, and the Intercollegiate Studies Institute (ISI) began working with Betsey on this project. Betsey insisted on expanding the lectures into a full-length book, for, as sympathetic as she was to the difficulties faced by many gays and lesbians, she recognized better than almost anyone how the proponents of same-sex marriage skillfully manipulated the rhetoric, monopolizing words dear to any American's heart: "choice," "right to privacy," "equality," and "freedom of the individual." Grasping the parallels between the movements for abortion and same-sex marriage in their clever use of rhetoric to obscure their shared goal of reducing or erasing communal claims upon the individual, Betsey strongly felt the urgent need to convince Americans—especially ordinary Americans—that behind the appealing rhetoric of same-sex marriage proponents lay a frightening new world in which all relations are "contracts or realizations of desire." Such a theoretical unpinning renders human relations by definition "temporary and volitional," and serves, ultimately, to liberate the "individual from all binding engagements."[2]

The goal of understanding the struggle of one against all—of the shifting meanings of individual and community, human freedom and binding obligations—had always attracted Betsey intellectually and morally. Her many books, lectures, and essays consistently wrestled with the questions that have always meant the most to humans. With faithfully elegant prose, Betsey turned her exceptional native intelligence, her remarkably intellectually rich upbringing (she was the eldest child of well-educated and culturally sophisticated historians), and her superior formal education (Bryn Mawr B.A., Harvard Ph.D.) to the service of seeking—without hesitation or fear—the truth, historical and moral, of human existence. In book after book, essay after essay, lecture after lecture, and class after class, Betsey toiled to uncover the truths of history—European, American, southern, religious, literary, women's—and to search within modernity's "escalating uncertainty and indeterminacy" for "a moral and ontological center" that would reconcile the "isolate self" with the obligations that bind one with others.[3]

That search carried her through a study of most of the modern West, from François Quesnay and the marquis de Mirabeau in *The Origins of Physiocracy: Economic Revolution and Social Order in Eighteenth-Century France* (Cornell University Press, 1976); to the relations between slaveholding white women and their female slaves in *Within the Plantation Household: Black and White Women in the Old South* (University of North Carolina Press, 1988); and to the intellectual roots and consequences of modern feminism in *Feminism Without Illusions: A Critique of Individualism* (University of North Carolina Press, 1991), *"Feminism Is Not the Story of My Life": How Today's Feminist Elite Has Lost Touch with the Real Concerns of Women* (Nan Talese/Doubleday, 1996) and *Women and the Future of the Family* (with respondents, Baker Books, 2000). Betsey also collaborated with her husband, Eugene D. Genovese, on *Fruits of Merchant Capital: Slavery and Bourgeois Property in the Rise and Expansion of Capitalism* (Galaxy Books, 1983) and *The*

*Mind of the Master Class: History and Faith in the South-
ern Slaveholders' Worldview* (Cambridge University Press,
2005). More of their collaborative work will appear in
the near future.

These publications represent only the tip of an ice-
berg: Betsey's curriculum vitae, which included her education, books, editions, lectures, book reviews, interviews,
opinion pieces, essays, grants and fellowships, honorary
degrees and awards, book chapters and forewords, editorial work, consulting, teaching, and works in progress,
fills more than twenty-five pages. Beyond the classroom,
the lecture circuit, the dozens and dozens of dissertations
she directed, the journals she edited, and the books she
wrote, Betsey's service led to our nation's capital, where
Betsey served for several years on the governing council of the National Endowment for the Humanities. Her
work embraced both the academy and the broader public;
she knew that the questions she investigated had implications that reached far beyond arcane ivory-tower dispu-
tations. All of her work testifies to the human dimension
of history and of contemporary cultural discourse—of
real people struggling to make sense of and find meaning
in their lives, struggling to understand rights and duties,
liberties and obligations, the claims of the past and their
responsibility to the future.

Betsey's unflinching pursuit of truth and her compas-
sionate respect for the dispossessed attracted many and
repelled some. Her long-time rank as a leading Marx-

ist-feminist intellectual who identified herself as a non-believer did not distract her from an abiding respect for the truth and the circumstances of real people's lives. Never, she once wrote, did she doubt that "a human life must have purpose, that each of us must serve something larger than ourselves."[4] Her own father, a lifelong atheist and renowned historian of European history, repeatedly reminded Betsey that "no honor or knowledge or worthy behavior can flourish in the absence of intellectual honesty, which necessarily begins with the most exacting honesty about oneself to oneself."[5]

Betsey's intellectual honesty had a profound and incontrovertible influence on my own life. I first met Betsey in 1991 when she was director of the nascent Ph.D. program in women's studies at Emory and I was a master's student in English at the University of Dallas. I knew next to nothing about Betsey, but a professor of mine, Melvin Bradford, described Betsey and Gene to me as Marxists—"but reasonable Marxists"—and encouraged me to meet her. I found Betsey easy to love and respect. A reasonable, warm, elegant, engaging, perceptive, brilliant, and charming Marxist, she managed—unlike most academics, male or female—to wear a well-cut suit with panache. Although I had been brought up by my intelligent, well-educated, Irish-Catholic parents to pray daily for the defeat of communism, I was also taught by my parents to respect and heed anyone who spoke the truth. So I recognized immediately in Betsey someone who valued—in herself and others—intellectual honesty, a virtue that demands the moral courage to see oneself with honesty. Betsey's honesty, which I immediately sensed, induced my trust. The seeds of our friendship, which was to grow for many years, began in that first conversation. And at the end of the meeting, pressed by another appointment, Betsey spoke plainly about wanting me to apply to women's studies. "But I have to tell you something," I nervously interrupted. "I am a serious Catholic. I am a pro-life Catholic. I would love to come to Emory, but I am not at all sure I belong in women's studies." "Nonsense," she told me. "You do belong here. And, furthermore, I believe in diversity, genuine diversity, in women's studies."

And so she changed my life. I saw, loved, and coveted in Betsey the same things countless others have cherished: her willingness to engage all others, the clarity with which she cultivated her own high standards, and her yearning to seek and embrace objective truth with moral and intellectual courage—astonishing qualities in anyone, especially a professed nonbeliever who had made her life in the very universities that have been on the frontlines of postmodernism and all its attendant values. Witnessing Betsey's moral courage and perseverance in the face of tremendous opposition and even persecution lent me courage to see what I could make of my studies of southern culture, of feminism, and of women writers, of how I could persuade my fellow students and professors—always with time, clarity, and consideration, as my mother had taught me and Betsey had modeled for me—to reconsider their own biases toward those with religious beliefs, especially Catholic beliefs.

About a year into my studies at Emory, I made an appointment to see Betsey, with my heart in my mouth, worried that I might shock her, but determined to confess my new status as founding president of Emory Students for Life. She congratulated me, chuckled at my discomfort, and told me something that to this day I hold and cherish: "If you cannot be who you are, than what the hell is the point?" Betsey lived that dictum. Her willingness to endure all sorts of unpleasantness—to put it mildly—for the sake of the truth transfigured her from the first-rate scholar she was born to be into something even greater: a woman whose formidable intellectual powers were wed to profound moral courage. In a ceremony in the Oval Office in 2003, President George W. Bush awarded Betsey the National Humanities Medal for "illuminating women's history and bravely exploring the culture of America's past and present. A defender of reason and servant of faith, she has uncovered hidden truths and spoken with courage in every chapter of her life." No wonder Robert George called Betsey a national treasure.[6]

Whatever Betsey intended to happen to her lectures on marriage is, in a sense, a moot point, subjugated by the unexpected and unbelievable. After a series of long and difficult hospitalizations following back surgery in October 2006, Betsey died at Emory Hospital on January 2, 2007, shortly before noon. Her death came four months before her sixty-sixth birthday, five months before her thirty-eighth wedding anniversary, and a month after she had celebrated the eleventh anniversary of what she called her "day of grace"—the day she was received into the Catholic Church and the day that her and Gene's shining full-hearted marriage was blessed as the sacrament it had always appeared to be. Her death, a hard and devastating sorrow, finished, at least, her terrible physical suffering. Betsey had had multiple sclerosis, a disease that had reshaped the last decade or more of her life, though she bore her suffering bravely and without a trace of self-pity. Betsey's temperament and will, strengthened by the grace she found in the sacraments, were cast from childhood by her parents' and paternal grandmother's extraordinary spiritual lessons, especially her father's belief in "the redemptive power of suffering and its necessary place in the life of any worthy human being,"[7] and his insistent teaching that "the greatest courage . . . is not physical but moral."[8]

In the last few years of Betsey's life, I witnessed her courage in fighting the good fight—physical and moral—without fail. And I loved her all the more for her tenacity and cheerfulness. But I fought her, too. I had long helped to organize her travel, and I knew better than anyone the exacting planning and negotiation that would necessarily go into any trip. Arranging her travel went far beyond dates and flights and dinner partners. Although Betsey could realistically accept only a fraction of the innumerable invitations she received every year from around the world, each commitment meant careful questioning of her hosts: Is there a handicap-accessible room available if she needs it? Is the room close to an elevator? Will there be someone to help her with stairs? Does the flight allow her space to stretch her legs, thereby minimizing the threat of thrombosis? Is there a comfortable chair and ottoman in the hotel room to facilitate her removing her leg brace? I thought she should slow down, forget the battles, enjoy picking books and gifts for my children, whom she had loved as her own, retire early and go to lunch with Gene, and fretfully watch her beloved Yankees. She disagreed. And she was right. Some lives—but not all—unwind peacefully, and Betsey left us with the consolation of the privilege of having witnessed a life well-lived and the continuing wisdom of her work.

I do not know if Betsey was blessed—or burdened—with a premonition of her untimely death, but she redeemed every living moment she had as best she could, according to her highest standards. From the beginning, shaped by her father's moral and intellectual teachings to the end, and with her heart finally set on living her life in Christ, Betsey lived out her vocation to love, no more fully than in her thirty-seven years of marriage to Gene. The novelist Gail Godwin wrote that in the best marriage "having each other make[s] more of them both."[9] In the best sense, marriage called Betsey and Gene to a life that helped them find their best selves and do their best work. They found in each other from the first a true and lasting love that only grew over the years and, as is the case with all good marriages, their married love nourished and sustained those others who shared in their lives.

Early in his priesthood, John Paul II wrote that "love is never something ready made, something merely 'given' to man and woman, it is always at the same time a 'task' which they are set."[10] Betsey and Gene lived out that noble task of marriage—and Betsey, intellectually, emotionally, and spiritually, understood as well as anyone the full benefits of such a lasting love, and the cost to us all of its failure. Such a love, Betsey understood, depends, in the words of John Paul II, "upon the contribution of both persons and the depth of their commitment."

As Betsey wrote in a fragment that was intended to be the beginning of this book's preface: "Marriage for love—the promise of an enduring and engulfing bond between a man and a woman—is a dream that refuses to die. In defiance of the rising tides of cynicism, sexual liberation, promiscuity (before, after, and during marriage), and declining interest in children, the dream still promises that we will finally be loved as we long to be loved." With the full force of her intellect, training, and faith, Betsey defended marriage, and she believed that ultimately our flourishing and even our freedom depends upon our own ability and courage to sustain and defend the institution of marriage here and now.

Part I

Marriage:
From Personal Bond to
Social Choice

1

Male and Female
He Created Them

U ntil recently, even the harshest critics of marriage never denied that, for better or worse, its nature and purpose have been to unite a man and a woman. Much of the rising tide of criticism leveled at marriage focuses precisely on the tensions of attempting to bridge sexual difference. Men bully, abuse, trivialize, and hopelessly misunderstand women. Women ensnare, emasculate, nag, and cheat on men. The litany goes on, and many of the complaints Archie and Edith Bunker launched at one another in *All in the Family* sound disconcertingly similar to those of early modern European folk culture or even Aristophanes' comedies. Among the gods of the ancient Greeks, Hera nagged Zeus, and Zeus philandered, strewing children in his wake.

These first three chapters will offer a series of vignettes intended to illuminate the changing social func-

3

tion of marriage and the current campaign to destroy marriage as a unique and uniquely valuable social bond and the essential cornerstone of cohesive society. Having originated more as a relation between families, tribes, or clans than as a relation between individuals, marriage has gradually been transformed into an exclusively personal relation—a matter of an individual's "right" to specific benefits and privileges and, perhaps above all, community recognition and approval. Thus, the institution that anchored and transmitted legitimate authority has emerged as the frontline target of a comprehensive attack on any notion of legitimate authority, natural or divine. The flurry of opinions on the crisis of marriage and the family obscures the magnitude of this transformation, but we can ill afford to ignore its implications.

In modern times, complaints about marriage have accelerated. Ironically, this growing dissatisfaction has corresponded with the most sustained attempt to link marriage to romantic love. Love and marriage may, as the song would have it, "go together like a horse and carriage," but by no means necessarily. First let us consider premodern forms of marriage, including the features that have provoked feminists in particular to dismiss all forms of marriage as blatantly patriarchal and oppressive of women.

Genesis tells us that God created woman and man for each other—"male and female he created them"—and enjoined them to "be fruitful and multiply" (Genesis 1:27–28). And woman He especially created as the true companion for man, who welcomed her as "bone of my bones and flesh of my flesh." The author of Genesis reflects, "Therefore a man leaves his father and his mother and cleaves to his wife, and they become one flesh" (Genesis 2:23–24). Disobedience to God cost Adam and Eve banishment from Eden. God told Adam, "cursed is the ground because of you; in toil you shall eat of it all the days of your life," and He warned Eve that "in pain you shall bring forth children" (Genesis 3:16–17). But even that original sin did not destroy their complementary natures as man and woman, and their expulsion inaugurated the fallen human history of marriage.

The Old Testament often offers a less than appealing picture of marriage, which helps to explain the outrage of some feminist critics. Beginning with Abraham, the patriarchs fathered children with concubines, took second and third wives, and frequently treated their wives as little more than servants. Even Jacob, with his many admirable qualities and his deep love for Rachel, during the years when Rachel seemed barren, fathered children by her sister Leah, whom he had previously repudiated to marry Rachel. Marriage frequently seemed intended solely to produce sons and to preserve the patrimony of the tribes of Israel. Thus, the daughters of Zelophead are told that they may marry whom they please, provided that they marry only "within the family of the tribe of their father," so that the "the inheritance of the people of Israel shall not be transferred from one tribe to another"

(Numbers 36:6–7). In a similar spirit, if a man dies without having a son, his brother must marry the widow, and the first son she bears him "shall succeed to the name of the brother who is dead, that his name may not be blotted out of Israel." And the house of the man who refuses this obligation to build up his brother's house will be called "[t]he house of him that had his sandal pulled off" (Deuteronomy 25:5).

In these passages, the importance of family and tribe demonstrably trumps the merely human relations of man and woman. Yet the Old Testament, like other ancient sacred texts and myths, also recognizes the force of love, which it frequently depicts as destructive. Men and women pay equally for adultery, to which both are considered susceptible: The man who commits adultery must be killed, and the woman with him (Deuteronomy 22:22). But in most other respects, equality falters. Thus, if a man dislikes his wife or finds some indecency in her, he may divorce her simply by putting a bill of divorce in her hands. During the period of the second Temple, a woman could similarly divorce a man. These rules eerily combine primitive and postmodern views of personal relations, in ways echoed in some of Toni Morrison's fiction. Disruptive passion, prototypically in David's obsession with Bathsheba and its brutal consequences, recur throughout the Old Testament, as do examples of devoted love between a husband and a wife. But the emphasis consistently falls on marriage as the foundational social bond.

What the Old Testament tells as stories and sets of rules and laws, anthropologists discuss as the forms of social life and social structures. Claude Levi-Strauss, the highly regarded French structuralist anthropologist, has argued that the basic roots of complex societies lie in the exchange of women. Primitive groups, like the early Hebrew tribes, are inclined to marry within the tribe with the goal, as Deuteronomy puts it, of strengthening the house. Modern societies frown on this practice of endogamy. As societies become more complex they begin to favor exogamy, or marriage outside the immediate kin group, and in many societies, including the Brazilian societies studied by Levi-Strauss, exogamous marriage typically means the exchange of women. In other words, the ties between two groups do not result from the vagaries of personal choice that might have sent a boy to another tribe while welcoming one of that tribe's girls in return. In patrilineal societies, men were held responsible for building the strength of the tribe, and women were effectively treated as bargaining chips to cement alliances or consolidate other political goals.

The role of marriage in the consolidation of political alliances readily appears in the history of ruling families. European ruling houses invariably married to realize political goals and would probably have sacrificed prestige if they had not. One of the most important examples concerns a marriage that did not occur: Elizabeth I, throughout her long reign, entertained a succession of suitors, each of whom she eventually declined. In entertaining them, she was dangling before them the prize of her person and her kingdom, thereby gaining large and small advantages for it. In refusing them, she was protecting her own position as ruler, which the presence of a husband would have compromised, if only by raising the question of her proper wifely deference to him. In the more usual version, the man was the ruler, which reduced the problem of domestic power relations—although it did not necessarily eliminate them, especially when the royal bride came from a powerful family. During the eighteenth and early nineteenth centuries, the Hapsburgs showed a special talent for marrying daughters for maximum political leverage: first the meddlesome Marie Antoinette to Louis XVI, and then the unremarkable but presumably fertile Marie Louise to Napoleon.

Marriage, as its critics delight in pointing out, has notoriously been used to further the economic interests of families, often in transactions that traded impecunious social distinction for socially lackluster wealth. Such transactions are as old as marriage itself, even when they are more symbolic than substantive. In sealing a marriage, the family of the bride or groom offered gifts and tribute to the other, and in some instances gifts were exchanged. The gift has figured as a powerful symbol in virtually all cultures—the tangible embodiment and confirmation of intangible promises and intentions. In ancient societies, the gift frequently took the form of a bride price—a sum of money, a bundle of goods, or even a specified number of years of work for the bride's family. Jacob, you will recall, having worked seven years for Leah, whom he did not wish to marry, worked another seven for Rachel, whom he did.

The traces of bride price and its more familiar counterpart, the dowry, persist in various forms in much of the world, although for significant reasons, which will become apparent, they have largely disappeared in the economically developed and highly individualistic Western nations. While the bride price is paid by the prospective groom's family to the family of the bride, the dowry is paid by the family of the prospective bride to the family of the groom. The logic is simple: In societies or social classes that depend heavily upon the labor of women and value reproduction, men pay a bride price to the families of the prospective bride for the loss of her services; in societies or social classes in which the status, wealth, education, or military prowess of men outweighs the economic value of the woman's labor and fertility, her family pays a dowry to his. Contemporary India offers a clear example. There, the two lower castes, which perform heavy labor, have retained the practice of bride price, while the two upper castes, which specialize in the professions, politics, and business, have adopted the practice of dowry—in theory to compensate the man's family for the cost of his education.

Since the Middle Ages, Western European society has favored the dowry, although women's labor long remained essential to peasant families and cases of outright wife-selling may be found as late as the nineteenth century, and American society has followed suit. Among the upper classes, dowries were often substantial, and the inability to amass them—or to amass an adequate dowry for only one daughter—could result in a young woman's failure to marry. Convents provided an alternative to marriage and permitted a young woman to leave her parents' home, but they, too, required dowries, albeit usually more modest ones than those demanded by the greedy families of eligible young men. Dowries also afforded a unique way to advance the social standing of a wealthy but not noble family. In a world divided into estates, which although less rigid than Indian castes were notably less flexible than modern class systems, a sufficiently lucrative dowry might suffice to move a young French woman of the third estate into the second estate—the nobility. As the practice spread, especially during the eighteenth century, it earned the quaintly inelegant description of "manuring one's fields."

After the French Revolution abolished the system of estates, the French joined the British and a growing number of European societies in the comparative fluidity of a class system that granted growing freedom to mere wealth in determining social standing. The impact on marriage, especially among the wealthier and better born, was immediate and is revealingly recorded in the great nineteenth-century novels. Those developments introduced a new, if seriously limited, measure of sexual "equality" into marriage, which opened new opportunities but simultaneously eroded the strength of marital bonds (the next chapter will more fully explore those developments). In short, marriage has secured a vast web of social, political, and economic functions.

Today, under the rising tide of radical individualism, those functions seem nearly invisible, although they remain considerably more important than most Americans want to acknowledge. The ideology of marrying, not marrying, or divorcing, all for love, throws a veil over marriage's more practical dimensions. Bitter divorces, prenuptial contracts, child-support payments, and custody battles serve as painful reminders, but the emphasis continues to fall on the quest for personal happiness. For most of history, the social, economic, and political functions of marriage predominated. In many communities, parents and other relatives played an important role in securing suitable spouses for their children. In India, for example, arranged marriages were the rule, and even child marriages were common. Yet even in circumstances in which individuals were positioned to make personal choices, laws that reinforced the relation between marriage and national sovereignty could thwart their intentions.

In the nineteenth-century southern United States, the Cherokee Indians, who considered themselves a sovereign nation, had strict laws governing marriage between women who were members of the nation and black and white men who were not. Since the Cherokee had a matrilineal society, membership could only be transmitted or conferred through a woman. Over the course of the century, the ability of black men to claim Cherokee citizenship through marriage to a Cherokee woman declined precipitously, as the Cherokee became more race conscious and more protective of their national status. They correctly viewed marriage as an integral part of their sovereignty.[1]

The combined weight of the social, political, and economic functions of marriage underscores its significance as the foundational social unit. To grasp the relevant perspective demands an extraordinary effort of imagination from those steeped in modern and postmodern assumptions about the nature of the human person and human relations. Some, notably the historian Colin Morris, argue that the individual and a conception of individualism appeared in England as early as the eleventh and twelfth centuries.[2] And there are strong arguments, although not those upon which Morris relies, that Christianity nurtured a specific conception of the individual both with respect to the quest for personal holiness and the sense of individual moral responsibility. Because of the slippery nature of definitions, it is ultimately pointless to quarrel with Morris, but it is essential to understand that most people in Britain, Europe, and throughout the world saw themselves primarily, if not exclusively, as the member of a group, usually a family first and beyond it a clan, tribe, community, or people—a race, as many of them would have said.

When so large a share of social order depended upon marriage, love could only be viewed as disruptive. Like Greek and Roman myths, medieval European culture abounded with tales of unruly and untamable passions, just as the more popular culture delighted in tales of cuckolded husbands. In *Romeo and Juliet*, William Shakespeare drew upon a rich tradition of consuming loves that defied the exigencies of political order and political enmities. The middle of the twelfth century witnessed the emergence of a tradition of courtly love that would culminate in the thirteenth and persist into the fourteenth century. Intended to soften and civilize the brutality of early medieval culture, courtly love inaugurated a new vision of love and prescriptions for the ways in which a proper knight should treat his lady. By definition, this lady, the knight's true love, was not his wife, but a lady of beauty and social position whom he served through acts of fealty and valor.

The cycle of Arthurian legends rapidly became a central piece of the culture of courtly love. Sir Lancelot's love for Guinevere, the wife of King Arthur, figures prominently in the cycle and doubtless influenced the other legends included within it. Among these, a special place belongs to the story of Tristan and Isolde, which did not originate in the cycle but was absorbed into it. According to the best-known version of the tale, written by Gottfried von Strassburg in the first decade of the thirteenth century, Sir Tristan is entrusted by his uncle, King Mark of Cornwall, to go to Ireland to escort the king's prospective bride, the Irish Isolde, to Cornwall. During the voyage, her attendant gives them a love potion, which instills in them an undying passion. Respecting the claims of kinship as well as social and political obligation, they remain on their assigned course: Isolde marries King Mark, and Tristan marries another, also named Isolde, but never consummates the marriage. Tristan's military responsibilities take him away, but after receiving a fatal wound he returns to Cornwall to seek Isolde, who had twice previously saved him from death. His jealous wife foils the plan. Tristan dies desolate, and Isolde, who arrives minutes too late to save him, lays down in his arms and dies with him.

Few tales better or more poignantly illustrate the potential conflict between love and marriage, which helps to explain why it has been so frequently retold. Among the many who have done so, we may note Paul Hamilton Hayne, Frederic Manning, William Morris, Algernon Charles Swinburne, Alfred Lord Tennyson, and Thomas Mann. Towering above all, Richard Wagner's opera, *Tristan und Isolde,* powerfully affected countless writers and painters in various countries and helped to consolidate the modern myth of *liebestod*—death for or through love. However flamboyant and informed by modern themes, Wagner's treatment captures the essence of the original medieval sensibility: Love is inherently dangerous and usually deadly. It is not compatible with social order and has nothing to do with the rearing of children, the predictable appearance of meals, or the observance of basic social conventions. Georges Bizet memorably captures the sensibility in Carmen's "Habanera," in which she announces that love is a rebellious bird—a child of the Bohemia—that has never, never known any kind of law: "If you do not love me, I love you. If I love you, watch out for yourself."[3] And Carmen's love, like that of Tristan and Isolde, ends in death. How could it be otherwise? Consuming, all-absorbing passion is inherently at odds with any form of authority, which its very nature defies.[4]

When authors like Kate Chopin, Willa Cather, and Thomas Mann weave music—sometimes explicitly Wagner—into their representations of love, they treat it as the equivalent of a love potion that takes possession of the individual's senses, with the same effects as an addiction or an obsession. In this trance, in which love reigns supreme, desire may fix upon any object, including a person of the same sex or, as Shakespeare, apparently eager to underscore the absurdity, suggests in *A Midsummer Night's Dream*, even an animal. The stories of passion weave a special web of longing, frequently drawing the lover—and the reader—back to the world of childhood and buried desires to merge with the mother in an all-encompassing love. These are the loves that, in Carmen's words, know no law. And it is in their very lawlessness that they depart from—and often threaten—marriage. It is, nonetheless, worth noting that in the medieval tales of courtly love, even the most consuming loves are not permitted to threaten marriage as an institution. At most, they can deprive a King Mark of a beloved wife, who dies of love for another.

To our modern sensibilities, the arresting feature of these attitudes may well be the assumption that marriage is not built upon—and may not even require—love, which obeys its own, frequently disruptive laws. Throughout most of history, Europeans, like most peoples, including the Cherokee, most Muslims, and the Hindus of southeast Asia, viewed marriage as much too serious and consequential a matter to be left to the vagaries of personal choice, especially when those choosing were mere adolescents. Marriage was the responsibility of adults, those who could properly evaluate the social, economic, and political consequences of a particular union. Early in the nineteenth century, when the idea of romantic love was gaining new momentum, Hegel, in *The Philosophy of Right*, defended arranged marriages. Planned by sober and dispassionate heads, arranged marriages had incomparably better prospects for survival than the rash unions of impetuous young lovers.[5]

Love might not follow from arranged marriages, although Hegel thought that more often than not it would, primarily because the prior agreement between the two families and the shared social context would give the young couple an additional incentive to love one another. They were taking their place in a social network. One way or the other, love had little to do with anything of importance, and it could always be accommodated on the side, as a wide array of elite men—and no few elite women—understood. In premodern hierarchical societies, married men might pursue one or more liaisons with women of their own class or dally with women of the lower classes or both. Kings regularly had what the French called a *maîtresse en titre*, and not infrequently other, lesser amusements on the side. Women, not least because of the risk of pregnancy, enjoyed somewhat less freedom in this regard, but many engaged in sequential or simultaneous affairs of their own, either while married or after a husband's death.

In one way or another, all of the players in this premodern social drama understood the importance of marriage to the social, economic, and political context of their lives—and to the cohesion of their society. Eudora Welty joked about Southerners that the first question they would ask upon meeting a newcomer was, "Who are your people and where are you from?" followed closely by "and which church do you attend?" In the premodern world of clans and tribes, one's people carried even greater significance, for family grounded and defined what today is known as the individual's "identity." The self was understood as the articulation or expression of the group, which was viewed as prior to it, not as an "autonomous" being that could assume and discard commitments at will. The reasons were preeminently practical: Survival as a lone or independent individual remained tremendously difficult for men and virtually impossible for women. Access to food, to shelter from the elements, and to protection from human and animal marauders was a problem for most people throughout the globe. Marriages bound peasants and villagers, as well as nobles and kings, into indispensable social, economic, and political alliances.

Throughout Catholic Europe, and in much of Protestant Europe as well, during the many centuries before the advent of secular state census records, the church kept the official records of a person's existence and, in this respect, ranked as the premier custodian of marriage. Dowries, which retained considerable importance, and inventories of household goods, wills, and other legal matters pertaining to the use and transmission of property were handled by notaries, who kept extensive records of them. But marriage, birth, and death fell to the preserve of the church, and in the eyes of the church marriage was a sacrament. Not until 1786, on the eve of the French Revolution, were Protestant marriages recognized in France, and even then Jewish and Muslim marriages were not. In France and elsewhere, the advent of a full-blown secular state heralded the recognition of civil marriage, but throughout the world religious marriage retained its pre-

dominance. Just as the Torah and the Bible were taken
to govern marriage for Jews and Christians, so was shari'a
taken to govern marriage for Muslims.

Today, we are awash in complaints against traditional
religious marriage codes. Feminists have taken the lead
in protesting their assumptions and provisions, primarily
because of their alleged subordination of women. And,
to give the feminist devil her due, traditional religions
do, at their best, place a woman under the control and
direction of her husband and, at their worst, legitimate
both his abuse and his abandonment of her. Earlier, in
discussing God's punishment for Eve upon her expulsion
from Eden, I left out the part, "Yet your desire shall be
for your husband, and he shall rule over you" (Genesis
3:16). And by now, we have been well schooled by feminist critics in the countless instances in which both Old
and New Testaments seem to promote men's domination
of women. Those same critics, however, have also turned
at least to the texts of the New Testament to prove that
Christianity favors the equality of women and men. Mer-
cifully, my purposes here do not include a resolution of
those apparent contradictions.

Premodern marriages throughout the globe have disproportionately favored the domination or "headship" of
men. Our forebears in virtually every culture have tolerated a husband's beating—or chastising—of his wife,
many have tolerated his taking more than one wife,
no few have allowed him to repudiate her if she fails to

bear children (male infertility seems to have exceeded their imaginative grasp), and virtually all have regarded men—fathers, brothers, sons who have come of age—as her natural representative in the public sphere. In short, traditional religions have concurred with traditional political regimes in viewing the man as the natural head of the household. This attribution of authority alone has been enough to lead feminist women and sympathetic men to regard the very idea of sexual difference with suspicion—if not outright hostility. Yet their response misses an important point. Head of household though he might be, the husband and father was also its delegate, and, in his absence, his place could be filled by the next senior member of the household, normally his wife, if none of his sons had come of age.

We have no justification for seeking sexual symmetry in some mythic golden age and then blaming some putative rise of patriarchy for the imprisonment and brutalization of women within marriage. Quests for a matriarchal past have proved fruitless, although there have been a number of matrilineal societies, including the Cherokee. One culture and religion after another, notwithstanding differences on countless matters, have adopted the same foundational premises. First, the human species divides into males and females who are at once mutually attracted and sufficiently different to be mutually antagonistic, but whose cooperation is necessary to the perpetuation of the human race. Marriage binds them together into what

Willa Cather brilliantly called a state of mortal enmity as well as into the bonds of sacramental love. Second, and more importantly, from the perspective of civilization and the species, marriage proposes a reconciliation of the most fundamental natural difference among human beings—sex. For to flee from engaging that difference is ultimately to flee from all the others.

It might make us thoughtful that, in broad historical perspective, marriage has not been about the gratification—much less the rights—of the individual but about the good of society. Armed with postmodern sophistication about change and the "historicity" of values and institutions, we as a culture seem to be rushing headlong towards the abolition of marriage as we transform it to conform to our personal desires. We seem to have discarded the reasons that previous generations defended it, notably its ability to ease the antagonism of sexual difference, to promote economic well-being and social stability, to ground legitimate secular authority, and to infuse the most important social bonds with a sacramental character. We still cherish—and even idolize—economic well-being, which we hold to the high standard of contemporary American prosperity, but we want no strings attached. As for authority, whether natural, secular, or divine, we want no part of it. And ultimately, the essence of marriage is the authority that derives from the acknowledgment and accommodation of the reality of difference, notably the fundamental sexual difference between women and men.

2

Different or Equal?
The Compromise of
Separate Spheres

Marriage has come under increasingly heavy fire, attacked especially by feminists, who depict it as the cradle and guarantor of women's oppression. Ironically, the form of marriage they attack is rarely traditional marriage, which they tend to relegate to outer darkness. Instead, they focus on the modern forms, which have contributed most directly to a growing respect for women as persons—and ultimately to the possibility of their enjoying many of the same opportunities for independence as men. In other words, their target is only peripherally the world of patriarchal power and arranged or coerced marriages. Their real target is modern domestic marriage, with its attempt to bind marriage to love and to provide domestic happiness for women. The late Carolyn Heilbrun captured their spirit of impatience when she wrote that marriage is "the most persistent of myths imprisoning women, and misleading those who write of women's lives."[1] Critics of this persuasion have little interest in premodern forms of marriage beyond condemnation of their "patriarchal" oppression of women. "Patriarchal" covers a multitude of sins and any historical epoch—which makes it easy to dismiss out of hand what are lumped together as "the bad old days." These critics see marriage as a license to abuse women, and they consider any view of marriage as sacrament or covenant a self-serving deception on the part of those who seek to perpetuate women's inferiority to men.

There are many problems with this picture, but for present purposes the most important is the fatally flawed understanding of the changes in the nature and function of marriage from the eighteenth to the twentieth centuries. Historians have fondly described these years as the source of companionate marriage, or marriage for love, which is held steadily to have gained ground. Beginning as a small trickle, companionate marriage swelled to a flood by the middle of the nineteenth century, at least if we are to credit fiction, journals, advice books, and even sermons and religious discourses. Men and women were intended for mutual affection and companionship, which they should find in marriage—and, if well bred, find only there.

True, the change occurred slowly and unevenly. Parents did not overnight lose the power to weigh heavily in young people's choice of appropriate partners, and even as their power to tell their children whom to marry began to wane, their power to tell them whom not to marry remained daunting, seconded as it was by the power of the purse. Love gained in respectability in relation to marriage, but if young people—especially those from "good" families—were encouraged to let love guide their choice of mate, it was understood that they would only choose within a restricted circle. That is, in a social circle that contained a pool of ten eligible young men, a young woman was free to choose the one she preferred. She was not free to choose beyond it. Even after monarchies crumbled under pressures for representative government, and after the privileges of the nobility lost some of their social power, marriage remained central to a variety of social, economic, and even political alliances.

The rise of the novel as a literary genre, especially in Great Britain, charted these developments with exceptional precision and clarity. It would appear that much of Heilbrun's anger at the story of marriage derives from her familiarity with British novels, which, from the middle of the eighteenth century to the end of the nineteenth, were disproportionately concerned with marriage. For feminist literary critics, men as well as women, this "master" plot, as it has been called—without, I think, the pun intended—was primarily seen as a way to enforce the subordination of women by teaching them that marriage, followed by domestic confinement and subservience, constituted the central purpose of their lives. Rachel Blau DuPlessis expresses the sentiments of many when she writes, "Once upon a time, the end, the rightful end, of women in novels was social—successful courtship, marriage—or judgmental of her sexual and social failure—death."[2] Heilbrun, DuPlessis, and the many who share their views have a point, but they give that point the narrowest possible reading. Nineteenth-century marriage in much of the world did constrain women's freedom in a myriad of ways, but, at least in Britain and the United States, it also granted women new forms of dignity and independence.

First, a word about intellectual and political context. The novel came of age during the two centuries that followed the English Revolution and included the American, French, and Haitian revolutions. While men and women fought for political independence and the abolition of a variety of oppressive social arrangements—most notably in the Haitian case, slavery—a variety of political, social, and economic theorists pondered the proper relations between man and society. Some of these intellectual reflections and debates focused on the problem of the individual: the freedom he—and, more rarely, she—should enjoy and the measure of equality that should prevail among individuals. Marriage did not escape scrutiny, especially since it was generally regarded as the cornerstone of society, and, however inadvertently, some of the leading theorists explored new ideas about it.

Writing during the English Revolution, Thomas Hobbes and John Locke in particular grasped that a viable theory of sovereignty must begin with marriage. And though they disagreed on almost every other point, they agreed that in the state of nature a man and a woman are equals in marriage.

Hobbes and Locke were constructing theoretical models of the social contract rather than describing and analyzing the world around them, but both were trying to understand the implications of a change in the nature of sovereignty in political life for the personal relations of the family. From different premises, they arrived at radically different conclusions. Hobbes, shuddering at the "warre of all against all" implied by political individualism, favored an absolute sovereign to whom all individuals would be equally subject. Locke, who had a more optimistic view of human nature and a greater commitment to the protection of wealth, favored limited representation in which participation would be determined by the extent of an individual's property. Differences notwithstanding, both goals directly challenged the multilayered hierarchical system of rights and privileges that had grown up over the centuries. Thus, not unlike the more radical revolutionaries who found it necessary to tear down before building anew, both Hobbes and Locke found it necessary to postulate a state of nature—in effect to wipe the slate of history clean in order to make a fresh start.

Here, the most important feature of their effort is the recognition that for all persons to be equally individuals, women must be equal to men—at least in theory. Today, we so take individualism for granted that we rarely think much about its origins, much less recognize its initial radicalism. Both Hobbes and Locke wrote in opposition to the patriarchal theory that joined religious and political authority in the claim that kings governed by divine right. Sir Robert Filmer, who wrote a treatise, *Patriarcha*, in response to Hobbes's secular justification of absolute authority, provided the most complete exposition of the assumptions that most people took for granted. *Patriarcha*, which argued that kings descended directly from Adam and enjoyed their authority by divine origin, was not published until 1680, after Filmer's death in 1653. In 1689, in the *Second Treatise on Government*, Locke attacked Filmer's argument frontally, arguing that sovereignty did not emanate from God but was inherent in the individual. Locke's argument transferred the locus of sovereignty and authoritative knowledge from God to man, but, as Locke recognized, it stripped away all justification for innate differences among individuals, including women and men, who, in theory, were now no more than interchangeable units of sovereignty and cognition.

Not surprisingly, the theoretical recognition of the equality of the sexes faltered at the door of the real world, in which such equality palpably did not obtain. Hobbes and Locke both found reasons for a woman to accede to the man's headship in marriage, thereby bringing their theories into line with prevailing practice. Neither could have foreseen that the individualism they ascribed to men would ultimately fail to provide a robust justification for allotting women a lesser status in the world. The justification of men's advantage over women lay not in political theory but in nature and revealed religion—and in, as Locke put it, "the laws and customs of the country."

The laws and customs of the country were slow to adjust, perhaps in part because marriage provided a welcome nesting place for fledgling male individualism. Adam Smith even claimed that the true justification for a woman's fidelity to her husband does not concern the legitimacy of the children she bears him, but "that preference she owes him above all others."[3] They also adjusted slowly because marriage was anchored and organized in social, economic, and political life. Incentives to promote the equality of women and men were few, especially for men, although women benefited from a rising enthusiasm for their special roles within families, notably in the rearing of children, but also in providing what the late Christopher Lasch, recalling Marx on religion, aptly called "a haven in a heartless world." But however great the increase in a sentimental appreciation of women, concomitant interest in expanding their economic and political roles did not keep pace.[4]

Like Hegel's owl of Minerva flying at dusk, it was only during the eighteenth century that Sir William Blackstone produced the magisterial codification of English law, *Commentaries on the Laws of England*, in which he wrote, "By marriage, the husband and wife are one person in law: that is, the very being or legal existence of the woman is suspended during the marriage, or at least is incorporated and consolidated into that of the husband: under whose wing, protection, and cover, she performs every thing; and is therefore called in our law-french a *feme-covert*."[5] Blackstone's views reflected the inherited wisdom of the common law, conserving rather than innovating. There is nonetheless a sense that the rise of individualism, at least in the short run of a century or two, placed new restrictions upon women's economic and political independence. For if a medieval wife could, in case of need, replace her husband as the delegate of the family or household, a nineteenth-century wife could not replace her husband at the polls. It is as if the rapid increases in commercial activity, economic production, and social mobility added renewed importance to the stability of marriage, grounded in the subordination of wives to husbands.

Jane Austen, writing during the Napoleonic Wars and on the cusp of the emerging nineteenth-century world of individualism, had an acute eye for the niceties and wrote of them with brilliant precision. Each of her six major novels features a bright and talented heroine, and each ends with that heroine's marriage to the appropriate man. Beyond that fundamental similarity, the novels trace the social trajectory of marriage over the span of almost two decades. In *Pride and Prejudice* (1813), Elizabeth Bennet, the second daughter of a clergyman who, through a quirk of inheritance laws, will not even be able to draw on his very modest wealth to provide adequate dowries for his four daughters, disdains aristocratic pretension. Yet, after appropriate plot twists and turns, she eventually marries the haughty Fitzwilliam Lord Darcy. Through Darcy and Elizabeth, Austen intends to reveal redeeming virtues in the aristocracy and to present a truly appropriate marriage as a way of revitalizing it. Darcy and Elizabeth marry for love, but their marriage represents what Austen views as important social considerations, including the need for some modest reform both in the effect of inheritance law on women and in the behavior of the less responsible elements of the aristocracy.[6]

Mansfield Park (1814) and *Emma* (1815), which followed *Pride and Prejudice* in quick succession, also explore the ties between marriage and social and economic change. So meticulous is Austen's dissection of social patterns that the British anthropologist Meyer Fortes used *Mansfield Park* to illustrate important features of marriage and kinship. *Mansfield Park*'s many lessons include a painful example of what happens to a young woman who marries for love with no consideration for the counsel of her family and friends. The mother of Fanny Price, the novel's heroine, had married a seaman, who could never provide adequately for their numerous children. Fanny, her daughter, is endowed with many fine qualities, but only after a protracted stay with her mother's wealthy kinfolk at Mansfield Park does she acquire the education and refinement that ultimately win her the heart of the man she loves. The happy conclusion demands that he also undergo a serious chastening, primarily by freeing himself from the seductions of a pretentious, pseudo-aristocratic woman and settling upon his true vocation as a clergyman. Here again, marriage is used to signify a mastery of the worst tendencies in the aristocracy.

Austen's exploration of these themes culminates in *Persuasion* (1817), her last novel. Decidedly more somber than the others, *Persuasion* launches the sharpest of Austen's attacks on the aristocracy. Whereas previously Austen had focused upon aristocratic excesses, abuses, and pretensions, here she raises the possibility that the aristocracy has become so decadent as to have forfeited the justification for its privileges. Anne Elliot, the motherless protagonist, had, in her youth, allowed her godmother, Lady Russell, to persuade her not to marry the man she loved. Captain Wentworth was a navy man and lacked sufficient fortune to provide properly for the aristocratic Miss Elliot. Several years later, he returns to England, and he and Anne find themselves in the same social circle. During the interim, Anne's father, Sir Walter Elliot, has proven himself so financially irresponsible as to be forced to rent out his family estate and move into rented quarters. Admiral and Mrs. Croft, the couple who rent his estate, are navy people and friends of Captain Wentworth. The novel concludes with Anne's agreement to marry Wentworth.

The years between Anne's refusal and acceptance of Wentworth have tested her in many ways. At the novel's opening—and well into it—she hovers on the verge of depression, and even as her world begins to brighten, she remains more subdued than Austen's other heroines. Anne's years of emotional isolation are sobering, primarily in teaching her that mistakes in judgment and undue attention to false values could have permanently cost her happiness. Anne's case thus represents a refinement in Austen's treatment of love. Perhaps more significantly, *Persuasion* offers a significant modification in Austen's social views. Her early novels all betray her deep disdain for mere tradesmen and her continuing quest to redeem the aristocracy and the country gentry as the foundations for healthy social values. By the time she wrote *Persuasion*, she had significantly rethought her position. Although we have no justification for seeing Austen's navy people as proxies for the bourgeoisie, she leaves no doubt that they do represent new money and new careers open to talent. Wentworth is well born, but the Crofts are of middling origin, and Admiral Croft, like Wentworth, has made his career and his fortune by his own effort and talents.

Anne's marriage to Wentworth symbolically legitimates this new, upwardly mobile class even as it undercuts the aristocracy's pretensions to a preeminence their behavior no longer merits.

In *Persuasion*, Austen also explores the claims of love upon marriage—especially in the choice of partners. Should the motherless, nineteen-year-old Anne Elliot have defied the advice of her godmother, Lady Russell, and impetuously married the young Captain Wentworth? Since Anne and Wentworth do ultimately marry, it is tempting to fault Lady Russell for jeopardizing Anne's happiness and to fault Anne herself, as Wentworth initially seems to, for the failure to trust her own instincts. This verdict may not be Austen's. Throughout her major novels, she treats marriage for love with great caution, advancing good examples and bad. Her pages teem with impetuous, light-headed young women who blindly follow the first glittering uniform that crosses their paths. The results range from humdrum to disastrous. At the same time, each of her heroines does marry for love. Presumably, the difference lies between an immature obsession and a love duly considered, but the line is always hard to draw. In this respect as in so many others, Austen ushers in a new era of ambiguity.

The revolutionary age that extended from 1776 to 1815 marked a major historical watershed, leaving few aspects of life untouched. One may plausibly argue that the emergence of companionate marriage occurred over a long period and should not be seen as a revolution. But the revolutionary decades coincided with the emergence of Romanticism in the arts, especially literature, and with a new conception of companionate marriage and domesticity. Together these tendencies seemed to reconcile the force of love and the institution of marriage, which the Middle Ages had seen as incompatible. The questions nonetheless remained: Could marriage domesticate the unruly force of love? And could passionate love survive the daily demands of marriage? Romantic artists bitterly protested the constraints of bourgeois respectability, which, in their view, stifled human creativity as well as passionate love. French writers of the early nineteenth century, notably Henri de Stendhal and Gustav Flaubert, created heroes who invariably found an unattainable married woman infinitely more attractive than the appropriate and marriageable young lady.

British writers doggedly continued to wrestle with what is known as "the marriage plot," usually treating it as the only plot. Charles Dickens and Anthony Trollope stand out as leaders in this regard, but George Eliot wrestled with the same questions as they. In the minds of these writers and those who shared their concerns, marriage held the key to a worthy social order. In this respect, they were as likely as the writers of the courtly-love tradition to see passionate love as disruptive and inimical to domestic and social peace. Gradually, Victorian culture disciplined Romanticism, curtailing the open expression of passion, especially sexual passion. Probably never as puritanical as it is often depicted, Victorian culture privileged a chaste domesticity over wild demonstrations of passion. Figuratively representing the home as a sphere apart, Victorian culture drew an imaginary line between it and the world.

Scholars have correctly protested the boundary between the separate spheres of home and work, but this boundary was never as sharp as the rigid models suggest and, more often than not, there was positive fluidity. Representations—whether in literature or political theory or the law—never perfectly capture the messy ebb and flow of everyday life. It would, nonetheless, be rash entirely to discount the notion of separate spheres, if only because so many people of the time subscribed to it. In theory, separate spheres ascribed the home to the woman and the outside world to the man, thereby associating the woman with love, morality, and nurture and associating the man with power, work, and competition. Thus, marriage, in joining the man and the woman, joined the two sides of human experience, which, by complementing one another, together made up a whole.

Today's feminists have vehemently protested this arrangement as inherently oppressive—nothing more than another campaign to subordinate women to men. They are not wrong about women's subordination to men in the world, but they miss the many ways in which companionate marriage and domesticity benefited women, especially those of the middle class. Responsibility for domestic life offered women a kind of apprenticeship in individualism, even as it alerted them to the ways in which they were being shortchanged. If things went well, a marriage grounded in love and companionship brought them warm relations with their husbands and, in theory, protection from the unsolicited attentions of other men. And a new self-consciousness about the importance of motherhood brought them a large role in shaping their children's minds and characters. But none of these advantages brought them the equality with men that individualism might seem to have promised and that feminists now claim as an absolute right.

The criticisms of companionate marriage and separate spheres are usually launched from the perspective of the individual. The Age of Revolution introduced an emphasis upon the sanctity of freedom that gradually spread from the political into the personal realm, and with it spread an ever-expanding current of anti-authoritarianism. The authority of a husband over his wife provided an easy early target, especially when it was widely known that many husbands abused their authority in countless ways. By the middle of the nineteenth century, campaigns were underway to permit married women to control their own property, to liberalize divorce, and to permit mothers to retain custody of their children should divorce occur. Other campaigns focused upon women's access to higher education and the right to vote. Still others sought general social reform, notably temperance, as a check on men's perceived brutality. Today we take the legitimacy of these goals for granted, but in their time and place many were contested, often on the grounds of the physical differences between women and men. At first slowly, and then at an accelerating pace, most were attained.

If we switch from the perspective of the individual to that of the society, the picture looks somewhat different. In most respects, companionate marriage and domesticity diminished men's power over women and loosened the bonds of marriage. The sexual division of labor by spheres had the further consequence of figuratively divorcing morality from power. So long as the marriage held firm, female morality and male power could act in concert, reinforcing one another. Any weakening of the marriage invited an increase in public and private irresponsibility. Power could rule public affairs, unchecked by moral considerations, while morality could preside over the home, devoid of the power to enforce its own dictates. Stripped of the "protection" of marriage, women faced a dangerous world with inadequate resources.

The problems become clear when we consider that the same developments that fostered the spread of companionate marriage wreaked havoc on the marital opportunities of various groups of poorer women. The rise of industrial capitalism—another great revolution of the revolutionary age—pulled countless working people from farm households into factory labor in cities. With harsh working conditions and minimal pay, life was often as "solitary, poor, nasty, brutish, and short" as anything Hobbes had imagined, and marriages became difficult to sustain.[7] In England, it was common for entire families to work in the mills and factories, since parents could not earn enough to support their children, and no one could even imagine a man's earning enough for his wife to stay home with them. The wonder is that, under dire conditions, so many seem to have clung to marriage as the bond that testified to—and sanctified—their humanity.

On the other side of the Atlantic, slaves in the American South were deprived of the right to legal marriage. Many did "marry" in a variety of ceremonies, but their vows, even when professed in front of a preacher, had no standing at law. Once married, even when they lived on the same plantation—many slave couples did not—they lived under a constant threat of separation through the sale of one or the other and the even likelier threat that one or more of their children would be sold away. Much has been written about slave marriage and its absence, and feminist scholars have even suggested that slave women enjoyed greater autonomy than white slaveholding women because they lived free of the domination of a husband. We may be permitted to doubt that slave women saw it that way. For if they escaped the purported domination of a husband, they assuredly did not escape the domination of the master who owned them. Overwhelming evidence suggests that slaves deeply regretted their inability to enter into binding marriages, and, with emancipation, most of them married at once.

The slaves' response to their experience confirms one element in Orlando Patterson's exaggerated claim that to be enslaved is to suffer "social death."[8] The slaves of the southern United States enjoyed many human connections from which they built a vital slave community and Afro-American culture. But the lack of marriage did subject them to a kind of social death because it severed the connection between their personal unions and society as a whole. Coming from tribal societies in Africa, they retained a strong sense of the importance of the social bond and understood all too well the dangers of trying to build a social order on the vagaries of individual choice. Companionate marriage and domesticity, notwithstanding their shortcomings, did attempt to ground a viable social order in the willing acquiescence of individuals to authority. The balance was fragile at best. The economic pressures were unambiguously centrifugal and would become more so. The lure of the gratification of individual desire would prove almost irresistible. And the feminist insistence that women must enjoy the same rights and opportunities as men would fuel an uncompromising attack on authority—natural, human, and divine.

To understand my remarks as an attack on feminism would miss the point. In many societies, marriage has subjected women to brutal and unjustifiable domination by men. More often than not, men had the right to beat, abandon, or dismiss wives who failed to produce heirs or to meet other male expectations. Even in the absence of brutality, men have controlled their wives' persons and resources, while wives have had little or no recourse. The history of marriage has not been a story of sexual equality, and most of its inequalities call out for redress. The injustice of the inequalities does not justify our forgetting that the history of marriage has never preeminently been a history of individual rights—for the man or the woman. The history of marriage has been one of binding differences into a common purpose in full recognition that the responsibilities of the two sexes will vary with historical circumstance.

From a feminist perspective, the strength of marriage has always varied in inverse proportion to the independence of women—usually to women's disadvantage. The companionate marriage that prevailed from about 1750 to 1950 offered women unprecedented advantages, together with some galling disadvantages. The freedom to marry for love did not necessarily include the subsequent freedom to develop one's individual talents, much less to live according to one's fancy. Edna Ponteillier of Kate Chopin's *The Awakening* (1899) offers the perfect case in point. Feeling thwarted by her husband and children, whom she loves, Edna forsakes them in quest of personal and sexual independence. That her quest ends with her swimming to her death in the embrace of the waters of the Gulf Coast only underscores the fragility of companionate marriage as a compromise between equality and difference.

Together with men, women ascended to the abstract status of the individual, but unlike men, they had scant opportunity to enjoy its public prerogatives. And the more they challenged men's authority within marriage, the more they eventually turned to the potentially more draconian authority of the state. Marriage has ever been an attempt, as it were, to square the circle—to combine personal and public purposes to the advantage of both. The results have always been imperfect.

Christians have had long experience with the challenge of "equal but different." Equally valuable and cherished in the eyes of God, men and women are enjoined to fulfill very different roles in the world. Christians have not solved the problem of equal but different, but secular theorists and activists, who are increasingly liberated from any limitations on the freedom and rights of the individual, have done much worse.

3

Marriage On Trial

On Tuesday, November 18, 2003, in *Goodridge v. Department of Public Health*, the Massachusetts Supreme Judicial Court, by a 4–3 vote, ruled that, under the state's constitution, same-sex couples have the right to marry—or rather, that denying them that right failed to meet "the rational basis test for either due process or equal protection." In the words of the majority opinion, "[t]he benefits accessible only by way of a marriage license are enormous, touching nearly every aspect of life and death." The majority concluded that the right to such benefits "means little if it does not include the right to marry the person of one's choice."[1]

The decision explicitly appealed to Canadian rather than American precedents, thereby following the trend set by the Supreme Court—and celebrated by Ruth Bader Ginsberg—in *Lawrence v. Texas*. The influence of Canadian law and policy on the decision is clear, but the language also uncomfortably echoes that of *Casey v. Planned Parenthood of Pennsylvania*, in which the justices soberly announced that decisions about the meaning—in this instance, the value—of life were purely personal matters. And as others, notably Robert George, have pointed out, the disturbing evocations of due process and equal protection run through them all. In effect the courts have usurped the authority of the political process, assuming sweeping authority to legislate by *fiat* how we should live our lives—all in the name of our right to personal choice, which they celebrate as equal protection and due process.

The language of individual choice or individual right has proven extraordinarily seductive both as an invitation to do as one pleases with a clear conscience and as a deterrent against disapproval of the choices of others, which are grouped under the preposterously euphemistic blanket of "lifestyle" choices. Lifestyle choices, it turns out, include every imaginable sexual practice, including a new addition—"questioning"—as well as those older preferences which, not so long ago, were known by such judgmental terms as incest, pedophilia, statutory rape, necrophilia, and bestiality. Some older ones, like fornication and sodomy, seem virtually to have disappeared from our vocabulary. Lifestyle choices also include the choice to abort or not to abort, to marry or not to marry, to bear a child within marriage or outside of marriage, to cohabit or not to cohabit, and on *ad infinitum*. Logically, there is no reason not to add to this list polygamy and polyandry. The notion of marriage as the union of one woman and one man has been dissolved in a flood of options, reduced to the status of one "choice" among many. And if the gravest and most sacred features of human existence are reduced to matters of style, why should we care which styles others may choose?

We have reached a precipice, over which many seem eager to plunge, some maliciously, others blindly: Having reduced the most intimate personal relations, including those that have been our most reliable social bonds, to styles, we have banished morality from serious public discourse. The insistence upon viewing the world—including all forms of social and personal relations—from a purely subjective perspective has led us to embrace, as the Court in *Casey* encouraged us to do, the comfortable position that the weightiest questions about the value of human life are matters of purely personal concern—to be decided by each individual for himself or herself. With moral norms for personal relations swept aside like accumulated dustheaps and cobwebs, the ground on which to oppose same-sex marriage has been eroding. In the previous two chapters, I offered a functional and evolutionary view of marriage as a social institution, and it would be easy to assume that my intention was to endorse it. What could be more natural than to reason that, since marriage has constituted a primary social bond in different societies, it is only natural for marriage to continue to adapt to changing social, economic, and political conditions?

If changes in the larger social environment account for and justify changes in marriage, no era could be more promising than ours for massive change, and it is hard to believe that the proponents of same-sex marriage are not counting on precisely that logic to carry the day for their cause. The twentieth century arguably witnessed as much change as all of previous history combined. It assuredly witnessed a more rapid rate of change than any previous epoch, doubtless most dramatically in the realm of technology, but no less portentously in the realm of social mores. Until recently, all of the most visible social changes have concerned women, whose accelerating access to the full status of individual has decisively undermined the bonds of marriage and the bonds between parents and children.

Nothing could be further from my intentions than to blame women for our current woes. Much in women's situation called out for redress, notably their subordination to men and their exclusion from countless opportunities for independent participation in the public worlds of politics and work. But the justice of women's basic goals does not automatically justify the consequences that have ensued from pursuit of them. No less importantly, women's campaign for greater individual rights and personal independence was almost always more symptom than cause of the great secular changes that were radically transforming the world. For example, women legitimately sought greater freedom within marriage, especially control of personal property or wages, and sought greater opportunities as married women within society at large, especially the right to specific forms of work. But it does not follow that the best solution to women's demands lay in easier access to divorce—or even in greater freedom from pregnancy.

Indisputably, easier access to divorce, artificial contraception, and the resultant radical restriction of pregnancies increased women's independence within marriage, their freedom to leave or to avoid it, and their freedom to pursue careers in the public sphere. But these putative "advances" decisively weakened marriage in ways that might have been avoided. Easing marriage bonds seemed appealing to many men, some women, and, in the long run, to employers, who benefited from the mobility of unencumbered employees. Especially after World War I, when women gained unprecedented social freedom and even the vote in several industrial nations, including Great Britain and the United States, the rapid increase in urbanization seemed to enhance the desirability of single individuals who could respond to new opportunities without the burdens of personal allegiances. This increase in urbanization also offered women growing opportunities to work and to live on their own. As feminists have been the first to point out, the opportunities for women during the interwar years left much to be desired, and improvement often had more to do with style than substance. But that reality made the apparent freedom of easier social mores and easier access to divorce all the more seductive—to cynical employers as well as to many women themselves.

For the rest of the twentieth century, the temptation to blame marriage for many of women's disadvantages proved irresistible to many feminists, and no few women who did not initially identify with feminism found their arguments convincing. Campaigns for no-fault divorce, for example, passed in many states with little opposition, although a few astute social analysts, women as well as men, called attention to the costs, especially for less affluent women and their children, who typically experienced a decisive drop in income following a divorce. But the real blow came with *Roe v. Wade*, which has since stood as the cornerstone of the liberationist agenda. Independent of the heated—and uniquely important—debates about abortion, which increasingly have pitted the sexual freedom of the woman against the life of the child, *Roe*, combined with the mounting impact of the pill, delivered the knockout punch to the notion that a man should be expected to marry a woman he impregnated. Not for nothing did *Casey* piously affirm that women had become accustomed to working to support themselves—the justices seemed determined officially to liberate men and the state from any lingering obligation to do so.

Quite apart from the consequences for born and aborted children, the consequences for marriage, compounded by no-fault divorce, proved devastating. The marriage rate plummeted, while the divorce rate continued to rise, dramatically so in states that granted no-fault divorce. Today a mere 44 percent of American adults live in a heterosexual marriage, the divorce rate continues to hover around 50 percent, and those who live to age seventy or older are likely to spend more years of their lives single than married. In the view of *Business Week*, America has effectively become an "unmarried" country. Meanwhile, the disintegration of marriage is increasingly endowing the nation with unparented children: 33 percent of all children—and close to 70 percent of African-American children—are now born to single mothers, many of them young, underemployed or unemployed, woefully educated, and uninsured. The cynical may find in these numbers a strong justification for abortion on demand, but those most likely to live the problem would probably differ. African-Americans, in particular, are beginning to see the uncompromising defense of abortion at all costs and under any conditions as a not-so-covert form of genocide.

By now, at least some will have noticed that I have studiously refrained from talking, except in passing, about the relation between marriage and children and the importance of responsible procreation as the major justification for marriage. I have also refrained from dwelling upon the charms of marital bliss, readily acknowledging that marriages are as likely to be unhappy as happy, to which I should add that even the most loving marriages invariably have bad moments, and some may suffer months, or even years, of tension and unhappiness. Finally, I have frankly discussed the evolution of marriage and emphasized the ways in which it has fulfilled different social, economic, and political functions in different societies and in different epochs. Perhaps most significantly, I have said virtually nothing about religious teachings on marriage. My remarks could easily be read as a capitulation to—if not outright acquiescence in—a relativistic view of marriage: If it works, if it feels good, why not? If individual happiness is the measure of the good, then by what right do we oppose individuals having what they want?

The short answer, as we are reminded every day, is that the desires of individuals conflict. Pray remember that Thomas More's *Utopia* postulates as stern a government as the one that prevailed in Calvin's Geneva. As in the case of slave women, who enjoyed freedom from the authority of a husband only to suffer the authority of the master, the illusion of freedom in one realm more often than not veils a more ominous authority in another. The greater social and sexual freedom enjoyed by college students today appears to result in more instances of "acquaintance" rape and even "domestic" violence than occurred when they were subject to more supervision and regulation. The unfortunate by-products of their increased freedom have included a veritable explosion of student-life bureaucracies, which, instead of imposing parietal rules, impose mandatory diversity training sessions and untold hours of indoctrination in acceptable attitudes and forms of behavior. Yet only the obtuse can fail to recognize that the diverse members of our society cannot possibly all have what they want at the same time, and in many cases not even sequentially.

Since the incidence of divorce rose after World War I, the emphasis on individual wants has grown ever more insistent. The boom of the 1920s promoted an unreal atmosphere of limitless possibilities, but the stock market crash of 1929, followed by the long decade of the Great Depression and then the four years of World War II, introduced a harsh dose of reality. The Depression encouraged, when it did not force, the deferment of marriage for many young couples, and if the onset of the war prompted many to marry and even to start childbearing, the real baby boom did not take hold until the war's close. The late 1940s and the 1950s blossomed into what many now nostalgically view as a golden age of family life, not least because the United States was also enjoying economic prosperity, unprecedented opportunities for home ownership, and a marked expansion in higher education, including for women.

The 1960s brought a revolt against this purportedly idyllic prosperity. The Civil Rights Movement led the way, but the student, antiwar, and women's movements followed in quick succession. As early as 1963, Betty Friedan had published *The Feminine Mystique*, detailing the woes of the middle-class suburban wife, imprisoned in material comfort, a stifling marriage, and mind-numbing responsibilities to children. In retrospect, it is striking that the beginnings of social and economic security for American workers, including unprecedented possibilities for African Americans, coincided with the first explosions of restlessness and boredom for middle-class women.

At the time, it often appeared that easier access to divorce was benefiting men rather than women, primarily because men could take up with a younger second wife, leaving the first with diminished financial resources, the responsibility for children, and little or no preparation for gainful, much less challenging, employment. One feminist novelist after another chronicled versions of this story, but, tellingly, the vast majority of them represented it as positive. However much the woman lost and whatever her initial fears and pain, she was represented as gaining a new lease on life—her first taste of the freedom to become truly herself and perhaps to discover a previously unimaginable happiness with a new marriage, a younger male lover, or even another woman. Beyond the pages of fiction, and not always within them, things did not automatically end so well, and in real life, they took a high toll on children.

The escalating failure of marriage since the 1960s may fairly be told as a story of the betrayal of children. In the United States, in which divorce affects roughly half the children who are born into marriage, it is often considered in poor taste to dwell on the negative impact of divorce. Divorcing parents are quick to reassure themselves that their children will be happier if their parents are happy—happier than if they had to live with parents who were constantly fighting. In most cases, they are wrong. Short of violence and abuse, most children strongly prefer to live with both biological parents, no matter what the parents' own preferences. Numerous studies have demonstrated the importance of the presence of a father in the life of a boy, and it now appears in such studies that the presence of a girl's biological father is the most important influence on the healthy development of her early sexual experience.

Judith S. Wallerstein, James Q. Wilson, Mary Ann Glendon, and others have argued that the cost of divorce for children may be prohibitively high. Following the children of divorce for ten years, Wallerstein found that "'half saw their father or mother get yet another divorce, half found that their parents stayed angry at one another, and half became 'worried, underachieving, self-deprecating, and sometimes angry young men and women.'" Meanwhile, "one fourth experienced a sharp drop in standard of living; few were helped with college expenses; and most felt rejected by at least one of their parents."

Thus, as James Q. Wilson, discussing Wallerstein's work, concludes, although some children have done fine after divorce, "most did not, and this problem persisted well into adulthood."[2]

The news about the harmful effects of divorce has not been welcome in all quarters. The very frequency of divorce has led some school counselors and social workers to discourage negative references to it, lest they "stigmatize" the children of divorce. Sadly, the children, who are the most knowledgeable experts on the subject, are unlikely to find anything surprising in the claim that divorce is hurtful to those children who experience it. More sadly yet, too many children understand that they were never the primary purpose of a marriage that was intended to further the happiness of adults. Many adults do nothing to correct this perception, and their preoccupation with their own happiness—whatever it may cost others—echoes the theme of obsessive love that dates back to Tristan and Isolde. My point is not to dismiss the importance of love as an incentive to marriage, much less the importance of love between man and wife. But I do suggest that, however beautiful and valuable the initial impulse of romantic love, a marriage demands considerable sacrifice from both parties, and the arrival of children demands even greater sacrifices from both fathers and mothers.

Our society has betrayed and abandoned its children. Their sexualization alone should be enough to indict our culture for terminal decadence. It is pointless to attempt to hold individual parents accountable for the countless ways—including unspeakable violence—in which children express their despair and frustration, or simply their bad character. Bad parents assuredly exist. But even the best parents have difficulty in holding their own against the forces of the larger culture, which has little regard for the intrinsic human value of children, much less for their distinct needs. The disintegration of marriage bears a heavy responsibility for the devaluation of children, mainly because we have somehow managed to reverse the time-honored sensibility according to which children were the fruit, gift, and blessing of a marriage. Our culture is more likely to regard them as marriage's trophies or its burdens and to reject them if they fail to meet expectations or prove too heavy to carry. And it does not help that the women's movement, in its campaign to free women from primary responsibility for children, has effectively demoted the care for children to work fit only for servants.

Traditionally, many societies saw children as the main point of marriage, and King Henry VIII was not the only king—or the only man—to repudiate a wife who failed to bear him an heir. In his time and long thereafter, the presence of an heir—overwhelmingly assumed to be a male child—was intimately linked to the transmission of a special form of property, in Henry's case a throne and kingdom, in most cases, land. Thus, although the power of fathers over children might be formidable by today's standards, both fathers and heirs were also, in some sense, trustees or stewards of an estate that had preceded and would outlast them. Not incidentally, previous societies were also very much concerned with the problem of reproduction in general. If male heirs seem paramount to some, the mere existence of surviving children was seen as essential to all, for their absence would threaten the society with rapid decline.

Today, these concerns rarely carry much weight, and few people probably even think of them. Property has become increasingly difficult to transmit and almost always takes the form of mobile wealth rather than land, much less a kingdom or even an estate that has been in the family for generations. For these reasons and others, children have lost much of their practical value. And this declining practical value may help to explain some of the disregard they suffer. But not all. For the deeper value of children—confirmed by so many couples' frantic recourse to fertility treatments—is psychological and seems to reflect parents' desire to perpetuate themselves, even if only in a single child. The problems arise when the desire for children does not translate into the desire to spend time with them, shepherd their development, and place their needs before the demands of the external world.

There are many reasons for the declining importance of children in many people's view of their lives, and nowhere is that decline more apparent than in the couples who choose to forgo children entirely because they do not want the interruption, bother, or expense. Sometimes, perhaps frequently, couples who decide not to have children simply do not feel themselves ready to shoulder the responsibility. In other words, to borrow James Wilson's formulation, they are not sufficiently "grown up" to embrace adult responsibilities.

I can foresee the howls of outrage: How dare I or Wilson or anyone else judge other adults' maturity and sense of responsibility? Such judgments bear a disquieting resemblance to the moral judgments that have been banished from our discourse. Yet when we consider the current plight of children in our society, moral questions insistently impose themselves. And those questions relate closely to the crisis in marriage, although not primarily in the ways one might expect. It is impossible to exaggerate our moral failures to children, but ultimately those failures are society's as much as individual parents'. We have indulged ourselves with a culture that puts the individual—"me, me, me"—first at the expense of all competing obligations. Under these conditions, binding ties dissolve into matters of personal choice that may change without warning or concern for the consequences to others.

The problem of whether adults do behave like grownups returns us to the problem of marriage. It would be easy, although not without provoking outraged dissent, to chronicle the innumerable, and sometimes devastating, woes inflicted upon children. But the exercise would only take us further from the core problem of marriage. The intimate relation between marriage and children has historically been an article of faith, and the Catholic Church teaches that a valid marriage must be "open" to children, who must be welcomed, treasured, and raised in the Catholic faith. But even the church does not say that the bearing of children constitutes the essence and primary purpose of marriage. Presumably confusion arises because of the emphasis on openness to them, including the condemnation of artificial contraception and abortion.

Notwithstanding the overriding importance of responsible care for children, who merit unconditional love, the essence of—and primary justification for—marriage lies elsewhere. Marriage is an intrinsic good in itself because it bridges the difference between the sexes, uniting man and woman in "one flesh." In the Catholic Church, marriage, like baptism and holy orders, is a sacrament that marks a sacred rite of passage—entry into a fundamental commitment that binds the individual to a larger purpose and community. And although marriage unites two distinct and morally responsible individuals, it is no more about the individuals than it is about their union into one—a marriage that unites and transcends their individual purposes and desires, which henceforth are to be fulfilled in, through, and in concert with the other.

One of the smartest of the many recent commentaries on the *Goodridge* decision and the future of gay marriage noted that ultimately same-sex marriage will prevail because these days too many Americans, in small towns as well as in big cities, know one or more gay people and often know gay couples. The more accustomed Americans become to knowing gay and lesbian couples, the more likely they will be to accept their right to enjoy the same opportunities for happiness as everyone else. In effect, although the author did not put it this way, the collapse of public moral standards and the vast expansion in the notion of individual rights are making it increasingly difficult to deny anyone's right to fulfill his or her desires, whatever they may be. In our revolt against the allegedly unjust and discriminatory authoritarianism of morality, we have lost any ground from which to draw moral lines.

The demands for same-sex marriage flow logically from the moral tenor of our culture, and nothing in that culture arms us to resist them. Above all, having first acceded to the primacy of the individual over any semblance of a group, we are now capitulating to the non-negotiable demands of sexual desire. Nothing, in this climate, could be further from the dominant cultural sensibility than the idea that sexuality *per se* and *pro se* offers a woefully impoverished definition or measure of the individual. As our culture has loosened the bonds of sexual repression that allegedly thwarted the development and happiness of individuals, it has increasingly succumbed to the notion that no sexual desire can be denied. If you couple this assumption to the notion that marriage exists only to serve the interests and comfort of the individual, you are left with few weapons against the advance of same-sex marriage.

In an ominous development, the largest corporations, according to *Business Week,* are beginning to understand and adjust to this trend. Some are now offering benefits to a variety of domestic units and, in the process, are effectively displacing marriage as a special relationship or union. The consequences of this tendency, combined with our "me, me, me" cultural ethos, will soon end in the destruction of marriage. Oh, marriage will survive as one "lifestyle" choice among many, but as no more than that. And, make no mistake, that form of survival will amount to destruction, which is precisely the goal of the activists who are fighting for the legalization of same-sex marriage.

Many Americans, who come to see same-sex marriage as just another step in marriage's evolution, will accept the public pronouncements that they are doing no more than supporting "fairness" by extending some valuable benefits to people of the same sex who happen to love each other and wish to live together without shame or stigma. What could be more innocuous? But for the hardcore activists, the real goal is the destruction of marriage as the union of a man and a woman. They aim to discredit all forms of authority—especially God and nature—that dare to tell people how to lead their lives. In the view of queer activists, desire, like love in Carmen's "Habenera," knows no law—nor should any be imposed upon it.

In the current climate, the appeal of their position is not hard to understand, especially since most of those who accept it do not begin to understand its implications. If anything, the defense of same-sex marriage looks like yet another logical step in the gradual increase in freedom for all members of society. And since activists, the courts, and the media overwhelmingly encourage this deception, we may readily understand that many people may come to see same-sex marriage as another blow against outmoded and illegitimate forms of authority—a blow for freedom and equality. Buying into this view, however, they will remain blind to the ways in which they are playing into the hands of vast governmental and economic powers. The freedom for gays and lesbians to marry will decisively contribute to disaggregating all of the remaining social institutions that provide the foundations for any collective resistance against political and economic domination.

Contrary to many prevailing views, marriage is not the seat of oppression but rather the last best ground for resistance against it. In binding men and women into loving relations and shared purposes, marriage acknowledges the reality of sexual difference even as it works to bridge that difference and lay a foundation for a vital and, yes, grown-up social life.

Part II

History, the Family,
and the Human Person

4

Women and the Family

1: The Signs of the Times

In Matthew 16:2–4, Jesus responds to the Pharisees' taunt that he show them a sign from heaven:

> When it is evening, ye say, "It will be fair weather: for the sky is red." And in the morning, "it will be foul weather today: for the sky is red and lowring." O ye hypocrites, ye can discern the face of the sky; but can ye not discern the signs of the times? A wicked and adulterous generation seeketh after a sign; and there shall no sign be given unto it, but the sign of the prophet Jonas.

Today, as a people, we show no greater ability to interpret the signs of the times than the Pharisees did during Jesus' lifetime. Our problem does not lie in the paucity of interpretations: Interpretations we have in abundance. But like the Pharisees, we seem unable to shake the premises and practices that produced the signs in the first place. Consequently, our interpretations rarely challenge the status quo.

Teen Violence

In the spring of 1998, two young boys in Jonesboro, Arkansas, shocked the nation by shooting four young girls and their teacher. Few, if any, Americans doubted that four children dead, felled by two of their own schoolmates, ranked as a sign of the first order. Jonesboro was not the first—and presumably will not be the last—of the school shootings that are marking the twilight of the second millennium. In the words of Nadya Labi, reporting for *Time* magazine, the news from Jonesboro marked "a monstrous anomaly: a boundary had been crossed that should not have been." It was, Labi insisted, a "violation terrible enough" to rob the president of his sleep and "to cause parents all over America to wonder if they were doing enough to wall away their children from the bad angels that can steal into young souls and stifle the knowledge of good and evil."[1]

Labi's language bordered on the hyperbolic, but she correctly captured the quality of horror that gripped Americans who were searching for a way to think about causes and prevention. Jonesboro mocked standard explanations: The school was not in the inner city, and the eleven- and thirteen-year-old shooters were not poor. If such a violation could happen in Jonesboro, why could it not happen anywhere? Suddenly teen alienation, violence, and nihilism began to look like the rule rather than the exception, and adults scurried to find someone or something to blame. The too-easy availability of firearms, including semiautomatic weapons, provided an easy target, as did the promiscuous violence of the media, especially television and films, and video games. Neither attempt to identify and regulate the villains of tragedy made much headway. According to the current interpretations of the Supreme Court, the freedom to carry firearms and the freedom to produce violent and sexually explicit materials enjoy the protection of the Second and First Amendments respectively. More to the point, both freedoms protect the interests of the powerful political lobbies that represent vast economic interests. Notwithstanding a flurry of rhetoric, our political leaders have so far refrained from any action that would significantly curtail the economic freedom of major political contributors.

Who or What Is to Blame?

The ready availability of firearms and the proliferation of violent, sexually explicit materials offer an inviting target for outrage and blame, especially since they may be viewed as external agents. As dangerous emissaries from the outside world, guns and pornography play well as the evil angels or alien spirits that can infiltrate the private sphere of the family. The infiltration is all the more alarming in the case of the Internet, which reached into the interstices of the family to claim children for its own purposes, and parents often do not suspect anything until it is too late. No wonder normally restrained people begin to see the influence of the Internet as analogous to the "possession" by witches or demons that worried parents in earlier times.

These "external" causes have wreaked more than enough damage, but in the end they do not explain enough. The broad dissemination of guns among young people has doubtless increased the probability that their confrontations will have deadly consequences, but we do not know if they are more likely than previous generations to engage in violent confrontations. Are we confronting a world in which young people have new instruments for playing out an old script, or a world in which they are following an old script? And, if the latter, how much is it shaped by the sex and violence with which so much of the media and Internet are inundated? During recent decades, tolerance of sexually explicit materials has risen dramatically. Explicit sexual representations and references abound in mainstream materials, whether print or celluloid. Even very young children may now be exposed to a bazaar of sexual practices, and the slightly older child may use the Internet to track down all imaginable—and unimaginable—forms of sexuality. American youth of all backgrounds are growing up amid this deluge, and it is difficult to doubt that it is shaping their sensibilities.

The public world of sex and violence has much to answer for; yet the focus on external causes has effectively forestalled close attention to the role of families. Surprisingly few publicly attribute the rash of young people's pathological behavior to the collapse of family life, much less to the tendency of mothers in particular to work outside the home. For good reason. Few are so lacking in charity as to condemn parents, especially a mother, for the rage or nihilism or despair of their children, although some would like to hold parents criminally liable for their children's criminal acts. Horrifying as the school shootings may be, there have not yet been enough of them to rank as a statistically significant trend. Perhaps the public has overreacted to events that should best be viewed as aberrant and, consequently, do not compel us to reform our society and culture.

Most commentators continue to avoid drawing direct connections between the aberrant behavior of children and the nature of family life, not least because a responsible connection is so difficult to draw. Any attempt to link school shootings to the nature of family founders upon the shoals of our ignorance about the specifics of parents' behavior and the ways in which it affects different children. Even when we have a good psychological understanding of family dynamics, it remains difficult to evaluate their causative role. Do parents "cause" children's behavior, and, if so, are parents responsible for it? Such a question may merit attention within the individual microcosm of a specific family, but it contributes little to our understanding of social trends. Yet patterns of family structure, dynamics, and spirit do affect those social trends, which they also reflect. Thus, even while it is impossible to blame a child's family for his or her behavior, it is entirely appropriate to draw connections between prevailing types of families and prevailing patterns of behavior among children and youth.

2: The Rise of Individualism

Discussions about the contemporary family abound, and they normally pit conservatives, who tend to defend the "traditional" family, against liberals, who tend to embrace a multiplicity of "family" forms and relations. Some of these discussions focus on the ways in which family relations advantage or penalize children, but only a dwindling number of participants on wither side has the temerity to insist that children would fare better if their mothers did not work outside the home, or, at least, if one of their parents were at home when the children return from school. These days only the most unreconstructed traditionalists—many with some hesitation—dare to suggest that a mother and a father may play different roles in a child's life and, hence, have different responsibilities. Indeed, notwithstanding currents of criticism from both the left and the right, our times manifest an astounding complacency toward the ominous tendencies of our political, social, and cultural life, for within a remarkably brief period we have, almost without noticing, embraced a cataclysmic transformation of the very nature of our society.

The Rise of the Individual

Today, Americans have endowed the liberation and the rights of the individual with a preeminence and sanctity that set them apart from virtually every other known society. Our unprecedented privileging of the individual has reduced the ties that bind us to society to a mere fiction—and a contested fiction at that. From a structural or anthropological perspective, human societies have originated and developed as communal enterprises devoted to production of adequate subsistence for their members and reproduction (or increase) of their population and culture. Throughout the world, growing social and economic complexity, notably in the form commonly known as modernization, has led societies to attribute greater independence to their individual members or, more commonly, to individual family units. Worldwide, the spread of capitalism has reinforced and sped the process of individuation, with the result that the idea of individual human rights is gaining wider currency in many countries.

The progress of capitalism and the ideology of individualism should not delude us into viewing the sanctity of the individual as a global norm, which it demonstrably is not. Throughout most of the world, individuals still depend heavily on kin for survival, and families still exercise considerable sway over their members. Traditional religions, most dramatically Islam, and strong states reinforce the primacy of group membership even when they do not always support the power of family. Even a minimal sketch underscores how anomalous our emphasis on the rights of the individual looks in global and historical perspective. And a greater anomaly: Our complacent certainty assumes it to be an inviolable norm. Our complacency has dangerously blinded us to the truth of our situation, for what we insist on viewing as normative actually represents a revolution, the implications and magnitude of which we have not begun to fathom.

The Individual and Religion

As a small indication of those implications, we might briefly consider the preponderant cultural attitude toward social standing of religion. Relying on a widespread misunderstanding of the First Amendment, we have rejected public worship on the grounds that it violates the freedom of the individual and the separation of church and state. We have, consequently, lost the sense of a common or shared faith, even in the general sense of the Judeo-Christian tradition. Respect for the diversity of religious belief may require such public agnosticism, but the cost is high, notably the loss of a generally binding code of right and wrong. Many commentators appear to take comfort in the evidence that Americans' interest in spirituality is flourishing, and so it is, in every conceivable guise from the Christian solidity of Eastern Orthodoxy to physic readings and New Age cults of self-realization. A recent poll further demonstrates that American women are turning to religion in growing numbers.[2]

Thus, during the past two years, the number of American women who claim that religion plays an important role in their lives has increased sharply. Today, three-quarters see religion as important, and half would like religious organizations to participate in public discussion of men's and women's roles in society. Almost half would also like religious organizations to participate in the public discussion of abortion, and more than two-thirds favor restrictions on abortion.[3] These findings offer reasons for optimism about changes in our cultural climate, but they also present formidable problems of interpretation, for the very women who acknowledge the importance of religion in their lives, even those who doubt the wisdom of abortion on demand, do not seem to view their church's teachings on sexuality and men's and women's roles as authoritative. The problem is not simply that women find their priests, ministers, or rabbis reactionary or punitive concerning women's roles. More than half the women who attend church believe their clergy favors equality between women and men, and more than three-quarters claim that their clergy offers instruction on what it means to be a good mother and a good wife. The real problem seems to be that many churchgoing women do not acknowledge their church's teaching as influential, much less as binding, on their own lives.

A mere third of the women who value religion and attend church believe that their church has decisively influenced their view of abortion, less than a quarter credit religion with an important influence on their understanding of marriage, and only 13 percent credit it with influencing their understanding of gender equality. At the same time, a large majority claims that religion offers them moral and ethical standards (88 percent), helps them with personal problems (85 percent), makes them feel they belong to a community (84 percent), and offers them opportunities for leadership (75 percent). At first glance, these findings appear confusing. What are we to make of women who believe that their church offers them moral and ethical standards but who are not influenced by its teachings on abortion, marriage, or gender equality? It seems possible that women primarily value religion for assistance with personal problems, a sense of belonging, and the opportunity for leadership. If so, we might conclude that they value religion for what it offers them rather than for what it demands of them.

These findings bear a strong resemblance to those of James Davison Hunter and his associates.[4] In their survey, respondents consistently resisted the idea that moral imperatives should govern disparate situations. Time and again, they refused to hold someone else to a moral standard when they did not know her feelings about her situation. Both surveys suggest that even Americans who view themselves as religious or spiritual resist the idea of religion's authority over their lives. In other words, they believe that the ultimate religious judgment emanates from the individual rather than from God, much less from his priests, ministers, and rabbis. The emphasis on the private reinforces individualism at the expense of the social bond, especially with respect to the claims of morality, which is reduced from God's commandment to a matter of personal preference or choice.[5] Yet no amount of private spirituality can substitute for public—that is, community, worship.

The Individual and the Family

Just as individualism has so permeated many Americans' views of religion as to transform its meaning, so has it permeated our understanding of the family as a unit and of relations among its members. Throughout much of American history, the family ranked as a foundational social unit and was, as Alexis de Tocqueville noted in *Democracy in America*, essential to the well-being of the country. Throughout the nineteenth and much of the twentieth century, the family ranked as the main social institution and enjoyed a significant measure of autonomy. Especially in the slaveholding South and the frontier West, but also throughout the older northern states, the family represented a kind of corporate enclave. Even within the bustle of the competitive individualism, capitalism, and democracy that were coming to dominate the northeastern states, the family remained tied to hierarchical principles that placed the man, husband and father, in authority over all, including his wife, and placed both parents in authority over their children.

The special standing of the family had a long intellectual and political pedigree that had marked it as "different in kind" or "distinct" form other institutions or associations. Similarly, the law, following these traditions, had marked relations among family members and of family members with those outside the family as both discrete and unique. In other words, family members occupied particularistic positions by virtue of their place within the family: They were husband, wife, father, mother, child rather than abstract individuals.[6] In theory, particularism promised that each member of the family could be excellent—or flawed—according to the standards of his or her specific role rather than in the abstract. By the same token, particularism undercut any claims to assess the relations among family members according to the standards of abstract individual right.

Women as Individuals

The first stirrings of the women's movement in the mid-nineteenth century inaugurated a long and ultimately successful campaign against the injustices of the subordination of women to men within the family. These early women's rights activists, frequently evoking an analogy between the condition of married women and that of slaves, gradually secured a number of reforms, beginning with a married woman's right to own property in her name. From the start, the most radical of them insisted on the importance of winning women full standing as individuals, independent of their family relations. Second-wave feminists even more sharply condemned the family as the cradle of women's oppression, and they successfully campaigned for no-fault divorce, recognition of marital rape, and other forms of assistance for the wives of abusive husbands.

Many of these changes represented significant progress for women, and few today would, I think, dispute their positive value, but there is also reason to believe that they have come at an exorbitantly high price. Their impact has been all the greater because they occurred in conjunction with—and arguably partially because of—a massive movement of married women and mothers of small children into the labor force. Thus, just as the formal bonds of the family were being weakened by legal reforms, the presence of women in the family was decreasing because of the time they were spending at work, and women's economic independence from their husbands was increasing because of the wages they were earning. Arguably, the most serious casualties of this slow dissolution of the family's corporate character are the children, who are increasingly being turned over to others or left to their own devices. Taken as a whole, these developments represent a massive infusion of the individualist principles and practices into the family and the attendant destruction of the notion of the privacy right of the family qua family—or the family as a corporate body rather than as an arbitrary collection of individuals.[7] Many contemporary commentators have celebrated these trends, arguing that "a family-based privacy right is out of sync with contemporary sociological reality," that "a family-based privacy right is both constitutionally and philosophically unsound," and that the notion of familial privacy should give way to a notion of privacy that "centers on autonomous individuals."[8]

Heated struggle over the rights, nature, and mission of women has marked the recent decades during which the most dramatic of these changes have occurred. Within religious as well as secular circles, these changes have generated intense and often polarizing struggles between those who demand the "liberation" of women from unjust constraints and those who enjoin women to reembrace their "traditional" roles and responsibilities. In practice, most women have rejected both extremes, preferring to adopt aspects of each in the hope of finding a livable balance between a measure of individual freedom for themselves and attention to their obligations and responsibilities to others. The ability of women to get on with their lives in the midst of this raging rhetorical battle might seem to suggest that the clash of opinions can be dismissed as much ado about nothing, but before we settle for that comfortable agnosticism, we should recall that the extremists exercise considerable influence on both public opinion and policy.

Angry charges from both camps abound, while none of us can confidently assess the upheaval through which we are living. Nor can we determine the measure to which the transformation of the situation of women has caused the upheaval and the measure to which it is another by-product of larger social trends. Or to put it differently, in what measure have women struggled to improve their standing as individuals because traditional structures are collapsing, and in what measure have their struggles accelerated, or even caused, the collapse? Doubtless, some of each, although the allocation of blame serves no useful purpose. The rhetorical battles have distracted us from the most significant aspects of the change, for independent of whether one approves the new pattern of women's lives, it is difficult to deny that the crevice that has opened between the lives of women and the nurturing stewardship of families and children has already had crippling consequences and portends even worse ones.

One thing is blindingly clear: The transformation of women's lives and expectations during recent decades has no historical precedent, and its consequences reach into every aspect of family and societal life. Above all, the changes in women's lives and expectations are having a radical impact on families and the very idea of the family, and therefore on the lives of children, and therefore on the character and prospects of future generations. Women are the bridges across which change passes between the individual and the world, and, these days, between the world and the individual. Fathers, too, transmit change in the world into the interior life of families, and we know that their contribution to children's lives is indispensable. But in our time, the change in women's public lives is proving decisively more significant and influential—although not exclusively in positive ways.

3: Feminism and the Struggle for Equality

One of second-wave feminism's great contributions was to encourage us to look at the family and society through women's eyes—to focus on and privilege the story of the individual woman. From this perspective, many social relations and institutions, notably the family, began to look a little suspect. It did not take much consciousness-rais-

ing to show women that they were performing a dispro-
portionate share of household and child-rearing labor, especially since they had known it all along. But conscious-
ness-raising and other feminist efforts did teach many to
view their contributions to family life in a new—and not
entirely favorable—way. Even those who were not pre-
disposed to regard the family as the cradle of women's
oppression were often inclined to chafe at the unequal
distribution of domestic labor between women and men.
Women's steadily increasing participation in the labor
force resulted in a growing resemblance between their
nondomestic lives and those of their husbands, but it did
not inevitably result in their husbands' assuming a larger
share of the burden at home.[9] And what was true with
regard to the division of labor also proved true in many
other spheres of life as well. Justice required that women
enjoy equality with men in all spheres of life. The precise
meaning of equality, which could refer to opportunity or
results, remained elusive and variable according to the
situation, but the ideal has acquired iconic standing.

At one level, the promotion of equality between
women and men appeared natural and overdue. Why
should girls not attend Harvard, Yale, and Princeton
like their brothers? Why should they not enjoy access to
professional schools in proportion to their talents and,
thereafter, equal access to the professions and equal pay
for equal work? Equality in the public world of education,
employment, sports, politics, and earnings gained broad

acceptance in a remarkably brief span of time. By the early 1990s, women were attending colleges and universities in equal or greater numbers than men, they were steadily increasing their representation in graduate and professional schools, and they were entering the jobs and professions for which they were prepared. Most dramatically, virtually across the employment spectrum—from McDonald's to Wall Street—entry-level women were earning the same pay as entry-level men.

Notwithstanding rapid progress, many feminists have found this growing equality between women and men in the public spheres less than satisfactory. By any objective criterion, the comparative improvement in the position of women relative to that of men has been revolutionary, vastly surpassing the improvement secured in a comparable span of time by any other working group in history. But it has yet to produce equal representation of women and men in the most prestigious and lucrative positions. Perhaps more important, the evidence suggests that most women are still unlikely to pursue careers with as much single-minded dedication as men. Consequently, women are still less likely than men to break into the highest echelons—to crack the glass ceiling—of business, the professions, and politics. In practice, these patterns testify to the persisting inclination of women to devote more time than men to family and children. But feminists do not readily countenance the possibility that women, in devoting more time than men to family and children, are expressing a preference. Many also find evidence of persisting discrimination in the tendency of women and men to adopt a somewhat different balance between domestic and public responsibilities, although overt institutional discrimination is becoming increasingly rare. Some continue to insist that hiring and promotion require more aggressive oversight and intervention; others focus on the need to make men carry an equal share of domestic and familial responsibilities.

Here, I have no interest in debating the specifics of these strategies, although I doubt the long-range value of either. In the interest of refocusing the discussion, I will concede that neither the public nor the domestic world is invariably fair and that men may, in any given instance, continue to enjoy an unfair advantage over women, just as some women may enjoy an unfair advantage over men. Nothing is more self-evident than the tendency of different economic, political, and ideological systems to advantage different social groups: Warriors did well under feudalism, entrepreneurs did well under capitalism, and so forth. Today, our obsessive preoccupation with equality between the sexes and with monitoring its progress or regress is distracting us from the nature and the magnitude of the social change that is engulfing us. Since the situation of women lies at the core of this change, women have understandably tended to perceive it subjectively as a function of their personal experience, and their subjective perceptions have effectively masked the larger underlying patterns.

Sexual Liberation and Its Influence on the Family

Take the case of sexual liberation. From the early phases of second-wave feminism, the sexual liberation of women ranked as a major objective. For many feminists, *Roe v. Wade* (1973) figured as the charter of the true freedom of women as individuals. According to this logic, the legalization of abortion liberated women's sexuality from the control of men. Finally free to control their own reproductive abilities by *not* having children, women would be as free as men to enjoy their own sexuality. If you credit feminists, legal abortion liberated female sexuality from the centuries-long domination of men. The freedom to enjoy sex at will and without fear of the consequences promoted women to sexual adulthood and autonomy. Defense of abortion on demand has remained a sacred tenet of feminists, who regard it as the cornerstone of women's sexual freedom and who oppose any restrictions on it. In this spirit, feminists campaign against parental consent for minors, spousal consent or notification for wives, a twenty-four- or forty-eight-hour waiting period between the decision and the abortion, or restrictions on late-term or partial-birth abortions.

Feminist campaigns to secure the legal standing of women as sexually autonomous beings have had dramatic consequences for the social and legal standing of the family. A woman's right to abortion had been defended in political language as an individual right—a woman's right to sexual freedom. No less significantly, it has been defended on the grounds of privacy. Consider the implications of these two positions. In the first instance, a woman has a right to be liberated from children—the possible consequence of her sexuality. This strategy effectively divorces children from any social institution by labeling them the concern of a woman rather than of a woman and a man. The second argument points in the same direction by reducing privacy to the privacy of the individual rather than the privacy of the couple or the family. As Mary Ann Glendon has argued, this interpretation of the right of privacy is a radical innovation in American law, and it represents a significant departure from the legal norms of Western European nations. Symbolically, the reduction of privacy to the privacy of the solitary individual effectively sounds the death knell of the family as an organic unit with claims on its members.[10]

Since *Roe v. Wade,* a succession of Supreme Court decisions on abortion has furthered the tendency to dissolve the family as an organic unit into a random collection of its current member. In *Planned Parenthood of Central Missouri v. Danforth* (1976), Justice Blackmun, speaking for the majority, averred that the husband could not claim the right to terminate his wife's pregnancy "when the State itself lacks the right."[11] By the logic of *Danforth*, the husband has no more stake in the wife's pregnancy than any other individual, which effectively strips him of any stake in the family and strips the family of any standing as an organic unit. More disturbing, as Tiffany R. Jones and Larry Peterman argue, *Danforth*, by shredding the husbands' stake in children, establishes that "there is nothing of one's own in the most serious sense left for husbands in the family."[12] In *Planned Parenthood of Southeastern Pennsylvania v. Casey* (1992), the Court reinforced the logic of *Danforth*, arguing that a husband "has no enforceable right to require a wife to advise him before she exercise her personal choice." Not merely does a wife have no obligations to obtain her husband's consent for an abortion, she has no obligation to notify him she is having one. In the Court's opinion, the notion of a husband's interest in his wife's pregnancy reflects "a different understanding of the family"[13] than that which prevails today.

In *Casey*, the majority of the Court explained the social and economic assumptions that informed its views: Women, the justices argued, had become accustomed to the free disposition of their sexuality and labor, and unplanned pregnancies should not be allowed to interfere with their ability to support themselves. The opinion amounted to a proclamation that the family has so decomposed that no woman or child could automatically count on its support, and an admission that no woman should expect the government to pick up the slack. If a woman can afford a child, she may decide to carry her pregnancy to term. If she cannot, she must have easy access to abortion. Feminists extend the defense of abortion as an individual right even to very young women on the grounds that a woman's sexuality is a purely individual matter. Such radical notions of individualism further undercut the view of children as a familial and social responsibility, effectively casting them as individual possessions to be disposed of at will. It should make us thoughtful that, on this point, the largest business interests and the feminist activists agree.

Critics and advocates of women's sexual liberation agree that the opening of opportunities for women and the sexual revolution have unfolded in tandem, but they differ about the consequences. Critics insist that women's rejection of their traditional responsibilities is resulting in the abolition of marriage, the destruction of family, and the abandonment of children. Advocates counter that the freedom to leave a marriage or never marry at all is essential to a woman's well-being; that the traditional family, "the cradle of woman's oppression," is being replaced by newer, healthier relations; and that children do better when their mother is happy and fulfilled. The passion of both groups admits little common ground and, especially, discourages a reasoned assessment of our situation.

The unfolding of the debate has made it difficult to deplore the consequences of the sexual revolution without appearing to condemn women. At the same time, it is difficult to defend the increased independence of women without also defending their sexual liberation. Yet the question remains: Does the increased independence of women require their sexual liberation? Or to put it differently, does sexual liberation strengthen the independence of women? Secular feminists answer both questions with a resounding yes and insist that abortion constitutes the linchpin of both. These questions do not much trouble opponents of women's liberation, for they find little more to applaud in the growing personal independence of women than in their sexual liberation. Under these conditions, it is almost impossible to criticize the sexual liberation of women without appearing also to oppose their increased independence.

What the debate in this form obscures is the close relationship between the sexual liberation of women—appropriately known as the sexual revolution—and the disintegration of the family. Contrary to the popular assumption that "living together" helps prepare a couple for marriage, couples who cohabitate before marriage are less satisfied with their partnerships and less committed to their partners than married couples.[14] If they marry, they are also more likely to get divorced than those who did not cohabitate before marriage.[15] The problems with cohabitation underscore the perils of sexual liberation for the women it purportedly benefits. Feminists dismiss the evocations of natural differences between women and men as evidence of repressive and stereotypical attitudes. In their view, patriarchal men have invented the alleged differences in order to perpetuate men's control of women. Yet recent scholarship confirms the age-old wisdom that young women and young men have different sexual agendas: Young men are much more eager for sexual relations with their steady girlfriends than are the girlfriends, who are primarily seeking emotional commitment.[16] The sexual liberation of women thus serves the interests of young men while compromising those of young women.

In practice, the sexual liberation of women has realized men's most predatory sexual fantasies. As women shook themselves free from the norms and conventions of sexual conduct, men did the same. Where once young men had been expected to respect a young woman's no, they might now plausibly assume that the no really means yes. They might err in the assumption, sometimes at the heavy cost of being accused of rape, but not because any social rules discouraged sex between unmarried young people. Where but recently a young woman's unintended pregnancy would have led to a shotgun wedding, it now leads to abortion or single motherhood. George Akerlof, Janet Yellen, and Michael Katz have demonstrated that the increased availability of abortion and contraception in the late 1960s and early 1970s led directly to the dramatic rise in births to single mothers. They plausibly reason that ready access to contraception and abortion seriously undercuts young women's—and their fathers'—ability to use possible pregnancy as a means to avoid sex before marriage or to secure a promise of marriage should a pregnancy occur. In this climate, increasing numbers of young women appear, however misguidedly, to have used sexual acquiescence rather than sexual abstinence to attract and hold a man. The skyrocketing number of out-of-wedlock births and the declining rate of marriage testify to their miscalculation. But the young women who tried to cling to traditional norms of propriety fared no better. With easy access to women who had no objections to premarital sex, men had no incentive to meet the demands of women who sought to trade sex for marriage.[17]

It is not surprising that young men who can obtain sex without marriage defer marriage or avoid it entirely. But men's preference for freedom over commitment comes at a price: George Akerlof argues that the decline in marriage among lower- and working-class men has led to the rise in crime, drug use, and underemployment and that these trends have a multiplier effect. As the percentage of unmarried men in a community rises, community acceptance of not marrying rises as well, with a concomitantly greater tolerance for the hooliganism of bands of under- or unemployed single men.[18] We need not minimize the toll that these patterns extract from the other members of the community, notably women and children, in order to recognize that the heaviest toll ultimately falls on the men themselves. Men like to think of themselves as dodging the "trap" of marriage, but marriage is, if anything, more necessary to their well-being than to that of women.

Marriage is also essential to the well-being of children, and children tend to increase the solidity of a marriage. But children are consciously and unconsciously discriminating: To them, marriage means their biological parents. Children who grow up in a household with both of their biological parents are, on average, better off than children who grow up in a household with only one biological parent, regardless of the parent's race, educational background, or even whether that parent was married when the child was born or whether he or she remarries.[19] Boys who do not live with both of their biological parents are twice as likely as other boys to end up in prison; girls are seven times as likely to be abused by a stepfather as by a biological father; both boys and girls who grow up with a single parent are two or three times more likely to have emotional problems and twice as likely to get divorced as children from an intact nuclear family.[20] These miseries do not begin to exhaust the handicaps that burden the children of divorced or never married parents. Children do not thrive on divorce or single parenthood, yet more than half of the children born in 1994 will spend some or all of their childhood in a single-parent home, and as of 1992, approximately half of all first marriages were projected to end in divorce.

Does Equality Put a Marriage at Risk?

At the dawn of the third millennium, the institution of marriage—and, consequently, the child-friendly family life that depends on it—is at high risk. A scant half of adult Americans live in heterosexual marriages (54.4 percent); barely one-quarter of all households include a married couple and children; almost one-third of all American children are born to a single mother (the figure jumps to almost 70 percent among African Americans); and one-quarter of American children live in a family headed by a single mother. All of these figures represent substantial changes within roughly the last thirty-five years. During that period, women's fertility dropped dramatically, while out-of-wedlock births grew by 26 percent, and families headed by single mothers by 13 percent.[21] Nothing suggests that these patterns will automatically reverse themselves in the immediate future, and we may reasonably assume that without a renewed moral and cultural commitment, neither marriages nor two-parent families will fully regain their standing as foundational social institutions.[22]

Contrary to feminist hopes and expectations, traditional gender roles and values tend to promote the strength and stability of marriages. Thus, couples in which men share domestic tasks with their wives are more likely to divorce than those in which they do not; those in which the man earns more than 50 percent of the family's income are less likely to divorce than those in which he does not; and the larger the share of the family's income the wife earns, the more likely her husband is to abuse her.[23] Many feminists have a deep stake in the idea of egalitarian marriages, believing that women will never be equal to men until husbands and wives share all responsibilities and have virtually interchangeable roles. Polls suggest that many Americans agree that the ideal marriage is one in which both husband and wife contribute to the family's income and to domestic labor and child-rearing. And empirical studies confirm that many married couples are indeed sharing responsibilities, although not always equally.

The erosion of the family as a distinct corporate unit has encouraged people to view marriage as a contract like any other and has fed the feminist insistence that the parties to it must enjoy equal rights. Unfortunately, the insistence on equality of roles increases the pressure on the marriage and often decreases both partners' investment in it. The equality of roles reinforces the idea of marriage as a contract and serves to protect each partner's self-interest as a hedge against divorce. Neither women nor men are likely to make compromises, much less sacrifices, for the good of the family as a whole if they do not expect the marriage to survive. And women are especially reluctant to put career temporarily on hold if they have reason to think that they—and their children—may have to depend on their salary. Yet if both husband and wife resist making a wholehearted commitment to the marriage, the odds that the marriage will fail increase. Mistrust feeds mistrust, and while both partners watch out for their individual interests, their marriages and their children suffer. The predictable divorce rate merely drives home the lesson that marriage and family life require a good deal more than the defense of one's individual rights. As Danielle Crittenden writes, the family "has never been about the promotion of rights but the surrender of them—by *both* the man and the woman."[24]

The emphasis on individual rights at the expense of mutual responsibility and service underscores the connection between the sexual liberation of women and the decisive weakening of families and worsening condition of many children. The point is emphatically not to blame women, many of whom have also suffered from these developments. The larger and, I believe, incontestable point is that the release of sexual taboos and protections that encircled women has effectively unleashed those taboos on society as a whole and, hence, on the lives of children who are not prepared to deal with them. The sexual liberation of women, combined with the feminist campaign against marriage and motherhood as the special vocation of women, has directly contributed to the declining birthrate, the proliferation of single-parent or single-mother families, and the number of children born outside of marriage. As women increasingly move into positions of direct professional and economic competition with men, they increasingly postpone marriage and childbirth or forgo them entirely. The growing economic independence of women also permits those who choose to do so to bear and raise a child without the cooperation of the child's father. At the same time, the ethos of sexual liberation has destroyed the stigma that condemned women for sexual activity outside of marriage. Many welcome these trends as progress for women, who are finally shaking off the shackles that bound them to dependence on men and thwarted their development as individuals.

Conservative women, in contrast, often campaign vigorously for family values but too often show no inclination to pay for services that might help less affluent Americans hold their families together. For better or worse, we have moved well beyond the point at which it is realistic simply to exhort people to do the right thing. Even many Christians have embraced women's liberation as a fulfillment of their personal and spiritual potential, and the calls for equality between spouses rings as loudly in many Christian circles as secular ones. The Christian emphasis on sexual equality in the family as well as in worldly roles confirms the pervasive impact of the sexual and economic revolution of the late 1960s. In effect, many Christians have embraced the spirit—and frequently the specific demands—of the secular discourse of individual rights.

4: Parents and Children

Francis Fukuyama has dubbed the cataclysmic sexual and economic revolution a "great disruption," which it incontestably has been. Many of Fukuyama's claims and conclusions invite debate and critical scrutiny, but one aspect of his argument commands serious attention: The new economic forces and systems that have come to dominate global life systematically erode institutionalized family life.[25] To be blunt, the new multinational economic giants have no need for stable families, which may actually interfere with their ability to manage workers and sell goods. Under these conditions, we cannot expect the world of production to foster the restoration of a responsible and ordered social and moral life. In the event of a crisis, political or social forces might attempt to impose order from above. But only organized religion—in the broad ecumenical sense—has the resources to promote and nurture a lasting moral renewal. Thus far, the mainstream Christian churches have showed little enthusiasm for condemning the disintegrative forces out of hand.

Fukuyama claims that people will instinctively back away from social chaos and generate new moral systems, and he finds signs that we are already doing so. He may be unduly sanguine. The popularity of Dr. Laura Schlessinger, however heartening, does not prove that a moral revival is underway. (Certain kinds of moral deviants seem to enjoy being spanked.) Individuals may respond to Dr. Laura's precepts and injunctions without substantively rethinking their individualist premises, notably their commitment to individual rights.

In the United States, the responsibility to embody moral precepts has always been disproportionately ascribed to women, who have been noticeably more likely than men to practice Christian virtue in everyday life. Today, however, feminism has taught us to view women's traditional responsibilities as a form of oppression, and as women "move beyond" or graduate from the practice of those virtues, we are left with fewer and fewer people who do practice them. We are not, I think, likely to bring society closer to the practice of Christian virtue by representing the practice of virtue as punitive confinement or oppression of some by others (women by men) and by identifying individual happiness with liberation from that alleged oppression.

Liberation from Morals?

Implicitly and explicitly, feminists have fostered the belief that the liberation of women must begin with their release from enforced servitude to children as well as to men. We have moved far from the sentimental pieties that enjoined women to find their greatest self-fulfillment in motherhood—the bearing and rearing of children. Popular psychology has led us from the painful recognition that mothers who lived vicariously through their children were likely to thwart their children's development to the self-congratulatory wisdom that children flourish precisely when their mother lives for herself rather than for them. No working mother willingly assumes the guilt that she is sacrificing her children's well-being for her own, and fewer people are willing to tell working mothers that they are harming their children. Most of us acknowledge that many women must work if their families are to make ends meet, and in many specific instances the children, understanding this necessity, also understand that their well-being does rank as their mother's primary concern.

The problem does not so much lie in individual cases, which vary dramatically, as in society and our culture as a whole, for the social, economic, and sexual liberation of women have flooded the dikes of prudence, propriety, and self-restraint that protected children from the most dangerous adult transgressions. Today, it has become common to condemn the hypocritical fiction that divided the world into public and private spheres, primarily because women's ascription to the private sphere served to bar them from the freedoms enjoyed by men. But this argument fails to acknowledge that the mores—fiction, if you prefer—that sheltered women and children as well. From the moment that public displays of sexuality and violence are accepted as inherent aspects of human nature, not to mention as individual rights to freedom of expression, they begin to penetrate the daily consciousness and experience of children.

Perhaps worse, the acceptance of public displays of sexuality and violence as individual rights effectively destroys the ideal of binding moral norms. By definition, when morality becomes a matter of personal preference, it ceases to be a binding social norm, and personal preference is merely the logical application of the consumer choice vigorously promoted by global corporations. The discrediting of binding social norms in turn undermines our ability to protect children, who themselves are now seen to enjoy virtually the same individual rights as adults. Thus do we fashion a world in which nine-, ten-, and eleven-year-old girls can reprove parents who attempt to censure their dress or behavior, defiantly insisting, "It is my life, and I can choose how to live it." Indeed, we have reached the point at which a television ad features a whining brat who badgers his mother unto buying him a toy while the mature voiceover intones, "Children get what they want, why shouldn't you?"

In welcoming women into the ranks of masterless individuals, our society has decisively privileged individual choices, dubbed "individual rights" over any conception of the common good.[26] With breathtaking cynicism, it has paraphrased the insidious corporate slogan "What's good for General Motors is good for the country" and announced that the common good consists of the sum of individual choices. The measure of our denial of the limits imposed by a common existence lies in our reluctance to acknowledge that choice inevitably and necessarily refers to what one forgoes as well as what one gains. Jesus left no doubt on this point:

> For where your treasure is, there will be your heart also. . . .
>
> If therefore the light that is in thee be darkness, how great is that darkness! No man can serve two masters: for either he will hate the one, and love the other; or else he will hold to the one and despise the other. Ye cannot serve God and mammon. (Matthew 6:21, 23–24)

Well may we protest that it is not "fair" that women bear the burden of protecting some conception of collective ideals, whether of prudence or of charity, but fairness in the sense of equal opportunity to sin is hardly the point.

Traditionally, Christianity has fostered a more nuanced view of the claims of individuals. From the start, Christianity emphasized the direct relationship between each individual and God, both his love for the particular individual and the individual's personal accountability to him. Indeed, the Christian vision of moral responsibility has always depended on an acknowledgment of the responsibility of each individual, who is held to love God and neighbor and who is judged for each failure to observe God's commandments. In this respect, Christianity introduced the very notion of the freedom and equality of individuals into world history.[27] In this equality before God's judgment and within his love lies the meaning of Paul's letter to the Galatians: "For ye are all the children of God by faith in Christ Jesus. For as many of you as have been baptized into Christ have put on Christ. There is neither Jew nor Greek, there is neither bond nor free, there is neither male nor female: for ye are all one in Christ Jesus" (Galatians 3:26–28).

Modern admirers of this passage too often forget that Paul did not intend to transform the standing of and relations among people in the world. Neither the Gospels nor the other books of the New Testament condemn slavery. Nor do they promote worldly equality between women and men. Paul cautions his listeners against abusing the liberty that they enjoy as Christians:

> For, brethren, ye have been called unto liberty; only use not liberty for an occasion to the flesh, but by love serve one another. . . . But if ye bite and devour one another, take heed that ye be not consumed one of another. . . . If we live in the Spirit, let us also walk in the Spirit. Let us not be desirous of vain glory, provoking one another, envying one another. (Galatians 5:13, 15, 25–26)

Firmly condemning "adultery, fornication, uncleanness, lasciviousness, idolatry, witchcraft, hatred, variance, emulations, wrath, strife, seditions, heresies, envyings, murders, drunkenness, revellings, and such like," Paul reminds the Galatians that they are called to "love, joy, peace, longsuffering, gentleness, goodness, faith, meekness, temperance" (Galatians 5:19–21, 22–23).

Fervent advocates of women's rights like to read texts of this kind as admonitions against men's ideas of their superior status, but Paul's words are more plausibly read as a warning to women and men, both of whom are called on to live their specific (allotted) role in true Christian spirit. Christian feminists frequently complain that men appear not to have taken Paul's injunctions much to heart. From the observation that men have felt free to ignore those claims it is a short step to the view that the principles of fairness and equality should relieve women of their observance as well. What proponents of this logic fail to acknowledge is that this liberation of women all but guarantees the triumph of people's "devouring" and being "consumed one of another." Others argue that men and women must equally work to restore the stability and vitality of families, and the argument is superficially seductive. In practice, many fathers are assuming a growing responsibility for the household and the rearing of children, and the trend is heartening. But the argument for equality is deeply flawed. In the first instance, we have the disquieting spectacle of the woman who effectively says to her husband, "I won't devote myself to children, husband, and family unless you do every bit as much as I do." Altogether more important, the argument for equality rests on the very individualist principles that are dismembering the family as a unit. In the end, if one takes the needs of children and the imitation of Christ seriously, "I want equal time off" does not cut it.

Christian Freedom

No person of faith or goodwill can doubt that women have too often carried excessively heavy domestic burdens and received too little respect in return. Today, many Christian churches are trying to rectify what they now see as their mistakes. Unfortunately, they are tending to take their models of justice to women from the secular world, thereby espousing premises that fundamentally contradict the tenets of their own faith. Consider the words of Mary Stewart Van Leeuwen, who informs "religiously committed people" that if they wish to defend the two-parent family, they should focus less on claiming the moral high ground and more on demonstrating through example their commitment "to egalitarian gender relations between spouses, to a radical degendering of both public and private spheres of life, and to the development of institutions supportive of childrearing that promote both female achievement and male nurturance."[28] Van Leeuwen, to her dismay, finds religious leaders sorely lacking in this regard. Yet she has taken her language and premises directly from secular feminism, which invites us to wonder whether she believes Christianity has anything to contribute to the discussion—or even whether the two-parent family has an intrinsic value.

Toward the close of Gail Godwin's novel *The Good Husband*, Father Birkenshaw, a dying abbot, tells his protégé, Francis Lake, "You know, Francis, just as the monks kept learning in the Dark Ages, it's going to be people like you who keep human kindness and charity alive in our."[29] Francis, who had left the novitiate to marry the flamboyant English professor Magda Danvers, is the good husband of Goodwin's title, and his virtues are those attributed by the Book of Proverbs (31:10–31) to the good wife: human kindness, industry, and charity—the virtues of service and sacrifice. Today, women are wresting themselves from the bonds of those virtues, and, as they do, the virtues are all but disappearing. Many—and not only women—do still practice service and sacrifice, but the injunctions to do so have all but evaporated. Increasingly, our culture at large is quick to see injunctions of all kinds, especially those previously directed at women, as signs of servitude, specifically, of women's imposed subservience to men. In this climate, few women or men are inclined to risk instructing women in their "duty" to others for fear of inviting charges of sexism. Godwin's genius lies in attributing those virtues to a man, thereby challenging us to see their grace and power without reference to sex.

The pervasive sense that women were punitively held accountable for the practice of the virtues of service and sacrifice has, more often than not, resulted in the conviction that justice entitles women to freedom from that practice. Women's freedom in this regard—whatever its positive contributions to women's dignity and self-respect—has led to a discrediting of the virtues. The logic seems to be that if feminists are correct in viewing women's "traditional" work as nothing more than servants' work, then only servants should be expected to do it. (Although how women then justify imposing it on men may deserve attention.) The demands and undeniable sacrifice imposed by those virtues tempt us to lose sight of their intrinsic value and to agree with the secular feminist verdict that they represent markers of women's oppression. Convinced by the spurious logic that women who lived under the domination of men were coerced into the practice of self-abnegating virtue, many insist that the liberation of women must begin with their liberation from service and sacrifice for others. Lost in this reasoning is the recognition of the centrality of virtues to the meaning of human life.

This challenge, however, is not one we are likely to meet if we continue to focus on the rights and liberation of the individual as an intrinsic good. Christians, especially, have always understood that the greater freedom is not the freedom *from* but the freedom *for*. As the chickens of our liberationist and individualistic priorities come home to roost, many women—especially, let us hope, Christian women—are beginning to understand that the price of radical individualism is too high. But many continue to choke on the notion that they might be called to somewhat different roles and somewhat different sacrifices than men. In our time, those differences are smaller than ever in our history, but the very similarity of much of men's and women's experiences in so many areas of life apparently makes the abiding differences more difficult than ever to accept.

The greatest danger of all may lie in the dissemination of sexual egalitarianism within our churches, for the core of Christianity has always lain in the simultaneous reality of our particularity and our universality. God does not love mankind; he loves each man, woman, and child, precisely for his or her particular being in a particular body. And he loves each of us equally because he is capable of loving each of us in particular. Our democracy insists on the separation of church and state, but that separation has never foreclosed a deep Christian influence on our political institutions and traditions. Now, as so often in the past, it has become necessary to renew that influence—to bring a Christian understanding of sexual difference and human equality to redress the excesses of the ideology of individual rights. And there would be no better place to begin than with the complementarity of women and men and their joint stewardship for children. Otherwise, we are in danger of mistaking the red and lowering morning sky for the red sky of a promising evening.

5

Thoughts on the History of the Family

Since the 1950s, but especially since the 1970s, contemporary concerns about the family have generated intense interest in the variety of family forms in different times and places. Recent decades have especially witnessed a veritable explosion of family history, ranging from oral histories of specific families to massive scholarly monographs on the family in specific periods to general interpretations and overviews. This work, at its best, has yielded fascinating results that have decisively expanded our sensitivity to the myriad forms which the purported transhistorical monolith of "the family" may take. Much of it, however, may fairly be viewed as suspect, if only because it was written to serve a specific political or ideological agenda. Above all, for what should be obvious reasons, many of the historical studies of the family originated in a desire to disclose the distinctive, if not unique, features of the family during the period under consideration and thereby to emphasize the difference rather than the similarity among families in different societies and centuries.

Not for nothing has the family captured the attention of historians: How better to expose an institution as the product of human choice rather than natural or divine order than to call attention to its historical variation? Indeed, during the years following World War II, and especially since the 1960s, historians have explored the multiplicity of family forms as well as the changing patterns of family formation and dynamics. Following the pioneering path traced by the work of the French historian Philippe Ariès, they have, for example, rejected the idea of childhood as a distinct and universal stage of development, insisting that the idea only took shape in Europe during the early-modern period. In earlier times, Ariès insisted, children had been viewed as miniature adults.[1] Others, following the lead of Lawrence Stone, have focused upon the changing character of marriage and its relation to the socialization of the young, beginning with child-rearing practices.[2] Most historians of the family, notwithstanding differences among them, have tended to follow the lead of Ariès and Stone in insisting upon the close association among the appearance of the idea of childhood and the emergence of the nuclear family, companionate marriage, and, especially, the modern idea of motherhood.[3]

Drawing freely upon psychology, sociology, and anthropology, historians of the family have, on the whole, emphasized the functional or economic character of marital and family relations. The broad functional perspective might be summarized as, "Each society gets the forms of marriage and family it deserves or which best serve its purposes." The economic perspective, which shares many assumptions with the functional, shifts the emphasis to the limits that economic possibilities place upon marriage and family, concluding that the nature of both are shaped by economic forces. Both the functional and economic perspectives converge in their emphasis upon the differences among families according to century, location, or social class. Both have, in this respect, paved the way for the contemporary or postmodern emphasis upon the malleability of family composition and the endless variety of family forms.[4]

The emergence of the contemporary infatuation with the infinite plasticity of "the family" helps to explain the fascination with family history. Having, in our own time, called the very notion of the two-parent heterosexual family into question, we seem compelled to prove that it has never been either naturally or divinely sanctioned and, if anything, to deem it more important that most people throughout history have been unwilling or unable to observe its norms.[5] Thus, the dominant tendency in family history seems to suggest that there have been as many kinds of families as there have been societies or even individuals. The logical conclusion to be drawn from this work is, accordingly, that the family, like the concept of marriage in which it is anchored, constitutes a relation into which people enter and that they frequently leave according to shifting individual preferences and interests.

In fairness, it is entirely possible that the attitudes toward the family and marriage that many scholars project upon the past may have triumphed in our own time. But, if we are to make any sense of the current debates about marriage and the family, we must understand that the situation of marriage and the family in our time is not merely new but unprecedented. For, until the very recent past, marriage and the family have been universally viewed as the necessary foundation of specific societies and of civilization in general—as the source and manifestation of human and divine order. This understanding of marriage and the family as the most important and abiding system of human relations, as simultaneously necessary to individuals and to society as a whole, has persisted throughout human history. Beneath the surface of changing patterns of marriage and family, the ubiquitous insistence upon the intrinsic value of marriage and family as fundamental goods for the individual and society has endowed the various manifestations and practices with a common character and meaning.[6]

Marriage and the family do change in response to broad social, economic, and cultural changes as well as in response to political and legal change. To take an easy example, where anti-miscegenation laws prevail, a man and woman of different race do not marry, even if they cohabit, and consequently their children enjoy no legal identity as members of their family. Similarly, slaves in the antebellum South could not legally marry, although they frequently entered into binding relations with a person of the opposite sex, sometimes with the blessing of a minister. And because these marriages had no legal standing, the children they produced were not legally the children of their biological procreators.[1]

The case of slave marriage throws into relief some of the central features of marriage and the family as legally or religiously constituted institutions. Today, many people primarily consider marriage and the family from the subjective perspective of the individual: Do they or do they not further the individual's happiness and fulfillment? Yet if, from the perspective of the individual, marriage and family constitute a subjective story, from the perspective of society they primarily constitute an objective story. Thus, the anthropologist Robin Fox reminds us that marriage figures as a central and enduring feature of "the network of relationships that bind individuals to each other in the web of kinship." And he argues that this network, like marriage itself, has functioned as "the pivot on which most interaction, most claims and obligations, most loyalties and sentiments [have] turned."[2] In other words, notwithstanding variations in form, marriage and the family have served as the primary link between the individual and society or the polity—the essential and irreducible social unit. In this role, marriage and the family typically secured the mutual rights and responsibilities of women and men, recognized the right and responsibility of parents to shape the future of their offspring, and secured the ownership and transfer of property. Until very recently, they preceded and outranked the individual, who was socially and politically defined by them rather than by personal attributes or status. Indeed, in the most important respects, marriage and the family, throughout most of history, have grounded and defined the identity of the individual, who is placed at high risk without their legitimization.[9]

At an accelerating rate during the late nineteenth and twentieth centuries, marital and family ties have increasingly come to be viewed as secular contractual relations, which primarily concern the state, if indeed they concern anyone other than the immediate participants. Throughout history, however, marriage and the family have been of primary concern to the church or religious authorities, who have viewed them as inherently sacramental. Until the French Revolution, for example, the records of marriages, births, and deaths were not kept by the state, but by the clergy, who inscribed them in the parish registers from which historians have drawn such valuable information. Throughout history, religious authorities have displayed a special interest in marriage, presumably because they, like political authorities, have viewed marriage and the family as fundamental agents and sites of the ordering of human life. And most societies have ascribed a primary role to the family in the religious and moral education of the next generation.[10]

Today, many dismiss the interest of religious and political authorities in the regularization of marriage and the family as further evidence of the curtailment of individual desire by illegitimate authorities. Others, seemingly in growing numbers, demand that religious and political authorities acknowledge, sanctify, or legitimize various unions between individuals or groupings of individuals as valid forms of marriage or family.[11] The mistrust of marriage and the family has especially bedeviled feminists, who are wont to charge both with primary responsibility for the subordination and exploitation of women. And there can be no doubt that the feminist movement has decisively contributed to the dismantling of marriage and the family during recent decades.[12] Yet religious and political interest in marriage and the family testifies less to the determination to oppress women and children than to a deep understanding that marriage and the family have everywhere constituted the fundamental social unit—the fulcrum of civilization, the threshold between nature and culture. The core of the religious and political authorities' interest in marriage and the family may, then, be presumed to have derived from their understanding that these are the relations through which people recognize themselves as human beings, through which people define themselves. The question was less one of their imposing marriage and the family upon naturally recalcitrant individuals than of their gaining legitimacy by associating political and religious authority with the fundamental social units into which people grouped themselves.

With respect to the bonds between marriage and family on the one hand and religious and political authority on the other, it is worth noting that both religious and political authorities themselves long borrowed heavily from the language of family relations, presumably because that language was taken to be the one that seemed most natural and legitimate to most people. The familial imagery that pervades Christianity begins with God the Father and includes not merely His Son, but also the Blessed Mother and the Holy Family. This same imagery pervaded and structured the early forms of European political authority, which, for centuries, depicted the monarch or the tsar as the father of his people. This form of political authority came appropriately to be known as patriarchalism. In its classic formulation by the British political theorist Sir Robert Filmer, it justified the authority of the monarch as a direct inheritance from Adam, the father of the human race.[13]

In theory, patriarchalism proclaimed a perfect symmetry between the governance of families and the governance of states—both understood to honor and obey the divinely sanctioned authority of the father. But variants of patriarchalism prevailed in societies that restricted its authority to the private realm and did not take it to justify the governance of public affairs. The leading example may well be ancient Rome, which endowed the father of the family with the power of life and death over family members and slaves. The power of the father in the Roman Republic thus exceeded even that of the power of the father in ancien régime France, who still had the authority to demand that the king imprison a son who dared to defy his wishes.[14] Even after the English had forcefully repudiated public patriarchalism and beheaded Charles I, the king who embodied it, they retained traces of its legacy in the assumption that a father would govern the family for which he was responsible, including his adult wife. Thus, in the eighteenth century, when Sir William Blackstone produced his great treatise on English common law, he insisted that in marriage the husband and wife must be one, and that one must be the husband. Blackstone was articulating the law of coverture, according to which the wife lived under the covering wing of her husband, who was held to protect her, govern her, and represent her in the public realm.[15]

The assumption that men naturally govern families, including their wives, has prevailed throughout most of history, although most premodern societies have granted more power to the family as a whole than to the specific husband and father, whom they have tended to view as the delegate of the family—that is, as the steward of an authority that provides for the proper ordering of the family as a whole, which transcends him as an individual. In such a world, it was frequently possible for a woman to step into that role and speak in the name of the family as a whole. Had that not been the case, Elizabeth I would never have succeeded to the throne of her father, and, although questions about the effect her marriage might have upon her role as sovereign persisted throughout her reign and may well have accounted for her never having married, as ruler she proved no more tolerant of challenges to her authority than he.[16]

Not all societies proved as faithful to the principles of delegation as the British, and to avoid complications, the French precociously established or rediscovered the Salic Law according to which a woman could never succeed to the throne. But elsewhere, notably Russia and Austria, women did govern in the name of their families, the interests of which they were believed to represent. Only during the modern and increasingly bureaucratic period did one country after another deem it prudent to institute explicit laws against women's political participation. And they invariably did so following the triumph of liberal, democratic, or individualistic principles that drew a hard line between public and private realms but also opened the way to women's claims to an individual identity independent of the family. Thus, during the second half of the nineteenth century, the United States and many, if not all, Western European countries explicitly barred—or tacitly excluded—women from activities and occupations. In this respect, a kind of sexual segregation emerged in tandem with the racial segregation that succeeded the northern victory in the American Civil War and the abolition of slavery.[17]

Feminists have frequently been tempted to condemn most, if not all, marital and family relations throughout history as patriarchal. Many even argue that an independent system of patriarchy, grounded in men's presumed universal dominance within the family, has prevailed in all times and places.[18] This charge woefully misjudges the true nature of patriarchy, which has been far from universal. More importantly, it fails to capture the complexity and, above all, the interdependence that have normally characterized the relations between women and men within marriages and families. To grasp the normal state of affairs, we need only remember that the vast majority of human beings have traditionally lived in peasant or farm families in which the contributions, including the labor, of the woman have normally been as important as those of the man.[19] We should also recall that historically most married women have lived under conditions in which the reproduction of the population was the first business of society, in which many pregnancies did not come to term and many babies did not survive infancy, and in which artificial contraception was not—or not generally—available. These were conditions under which the biological difference between the sexes had important consequences and were generally taken to justify significantly different roles for women and men, even when the women also played an important role in provision of the family's resources.[20]

To identify the principal common denominator among the various historical forms of marriage and the family, we could do worse than settle on the widespread belief that marriage and the family articulate the natural sexual division of labor upon which social order and civilization rest. So widespread has agreement been on this matter that, until recently, one would have been hard-pressed to point to a single system of belief (including the great formal religions), a single theory of government, or a single social system that did not regard that "biological" fact as foundational—as an expression of the natural law that underlies and sets limits upon the positive laws of specific states.[21] Only in the very recent past have we witnessed significant opposition to the view of men and women as different and complementary and naturally suited to cooperation within marital and familial bonds upon which the future of the succeeding generation is taken to depend. Indeed, had that purportedly natural relation between the sexes not encountered opposition, we, like other societies, would presumably still regard the family as the natural unit of all human society, notwithstanding differing assumptions about its precise composition and size.

Thus far, I have tried to underscore a few enduring, common elements of marriage and family at the expense of the various forms they may take. But historically, the family, precisely because of its pivotal and indispensable role in linking the individual to society, has demonstrated impressive adaptability: According to circumstances, families may be extended or nuclear, multigenerational or two-generational, matrilineal or patrilineal, matrilocal or patrilocal. They may assuredly be patriarchal, although they have probably never, as Friedrich Engels and others speculated, been genuinely matriarchal.[22] Marriages themselves have varied not merely by monogamy and polygyny, but with regard to whether they are arranged or freely chosen, established on the basis of a bride price or a dowry, and other factors. Scholars have emphasized the variations, in large measure, to disabuse the complacent assumption that to be legitimate family and marriage must always have observed the model we take for granted. All societies may attempt to ensure their own orderly reproduction through the ways in which they welcome and rear the next generation, but they have not all done so in the same way. Yet the very richness and interest of our new panoramic sense of the diversity of family forms risks obscuring the most important consideration of all. For it may reasonably be argued that none of these seemingly infinite variations matches in significance the sea change that has marked the modern and, especially, the postmodern world.[23]

If the modern ideals of companionate marriage and the nuclear family may not claim universal authority, they have nonetheless decisively shaped the ideas of contemporary Americans as well as Western Europeans, and, since World War II, they seem to have exercised some influence within a variety of "modernizing" societies throughout the world. The view of the family as appropriately nuclear and marriage as appropriately the product of the mutual love and choice of the individuals concerned emerged, as Lawrence Stone and others have argued, in Western Europe, notably England, at the dawn of the modern era. Scholars continue to debate the precise origins and causes of the modern ideal of marriage and the family, and most concur that it did not triumph in one fell swoop, much less gain an equal hold upon all social classes or even all regions of a single country. But they increasingly agree that, during the years following 1750, a new ideal of family and marriage was establishing a secure and apparently irreversible foothold among the English upper and upper-middle classes and that inhabitants of Western Europe and the North American colonies were following their lead.

Debates persist about the causes of the change in family size and dynamics toward the end of the early-modern period. Some scholars attribute the decisive role to economics and others to ideology, but most concur about the manifestations. The new attitude toward marriage emphasized the importance of individual choice and love rather than the preference for arranged marriage designed to serve the political and economic interests of the larger family. In conformity with this preference for companionship and love between the partners, there emerged a new attitude toward children and motherhood. Elite mothers, who had previously turned their children over to wet-nurses, nannies, and governesses, were now expected to nurse their children themselves and to play a major role in the development of their minds and character. These expectations typically arose more or less in tandem with the first stirrings of political individualism, and they derived from the new interest in children as themselves emergent individuals. Indeed, both political individualism and the new psychology of childhood had a common source in the work of John Locke, in which childhood was viewed as a distinct—and formative—stage of life during which children's impressionable minds and hearts were molded by the loving attention and firm discipline of parents, especially the mother.[24] Whether as effect or cause, these new convictions about marriage, childhood, and family life generally accompanied an older age at first marriage for women and a gradual decline in the number of children per family. And the whole was ensconced in a view of the family as a private sphere, safely removed from the hurly-burly of public life, and informed by the glow of intimacy and love.[25]

Most of us recognize this constellation of attitudes, if only because it prevailed among Europeans and Americans until at least the upheavals of the 1960s and still prevails among many today. What we do not so readily recognize is that this view, which so many of us cherish, contained within itself the seeds of its own ultimate destruction. Companionate marriage and the loving, child-centered, private family assured tremendous benefits to many people and to society at large, but they also created an array of problems, including men's abuse of women and children, the personal unhappiness of husbands and wives, and the psychic misery of children. We need not exaggerate the abuses, which have occurred in all families in all times and which may actually have diminished during the nineteenth and early twentieth centuries, but we do need to acknowledge them. In recent years, it has become commonplace—in some circles, obligatory—to denounce the repressive and abusive character of the "patriarchal" bourgeois family. But whatever that family was, it was not patriarchal, and it arguably served its members better than any known alternative.

Ironically, the very emphasis upon love and mutuality between husband and wife and among parents and children that fostered the best features of this family also opened the way to its erosion. For example, once one assumes that a marriage must be grounded in love, how does one prohibit divorce when love dies? By the 1920s, divorce had, indeed, become much easier to obtain and was beginning to lose its social stigma. Thereafter, especially in the United States, the divorce rate skyrock-

eted—all in the name of true love and the fulfillment
of individuals. The bonds of the nuclear family were
steadily loosening, but the decisive blow came with the
extraordinary sexual and economic revolution of the last
thirty years.[26] That dual revolution has spawned both
unprecedented opportunities for women and the modern
feminist movement, and has decisively undercut the social centrality of marriage. These explosive changes have
given us no-fault divorce, abortion on demand, rampant
unwed motherhood, and "children's rights," and now
threaten us with same-sex marriage as well.

The numbers that chronicle the proliferation of divorce, the children born to unwed mothers, the children
who live all or a large part of their childhood without
a resident biological father, and the other casualties of
our current attitudes and practices are staggering. But
there is a real danger that single-minded attention to the
quantitative magnitude of family disruption will obscure
the dramatic significance of the qualitative change. For,
seen in historical perspective, our contemporary situation is indeed something new under the sun. To be sure,
there are many who deny that qualitative change has
occurred, arguing, for example, that the proliferation of
divorce more often than not results in the formation of
new marriages.[27] And in truth, many if not most children
in the seventeenth-century Chesapeake lost one or both
of their parents before they reached their teens. Workers in nineteenth-century Paris frequently lacked the

resources to marry and lived in common-law marriages, which meant their children lacked legal standing. Until the twentieth century, most people died much younger than they die today, which meant that marriages did not last as long as those of today, and the surviving partner often remarried, which meant that many children grew up without either a biological mother or a biological father in residence. As for the contemporary reliance upon daycare and nannies, was such not the experience of countless children throughout history, especially among the well-to-do? All of which and more is true, but the use to which these facts are being put entirely misses the point.

For before the last thirty years or so, no known society has rejected some form of marriage and family as the ideal—and as a norm to which most people were expected to aspire. Exceptions to and violations of the norm were recognized as exceptions and violations. Today, if we credit our senses, we are witnessing a concerted attempt by a portion of the elite to deny the value of the norm. In its place, we are offered marriage as the personal fulfillment of the individual, who must be free to switch partners at will. And we are offered family as "families"—whatever combination of people choose to live together on whatever terms for whatever period of time. It is possible that adults may survive this madness, although one may be permitted to doubt it. It is doubtful that any significant number of children will survive it, as the mounting evidence of their distress amply warns. History suggests that, since the dawn of time, one of the principal tasks of civilization has been to bind men to families—to hold them accountable for the children they father and for the children's mother. The modern period slowly eroded elements of that accomplishment, while it introduced some salutary reforms. But it left the ideal intact. Since the 1960s, the postmodern elite has, as if with the snap of the fingers, exploded it. What may emerge from the wreckage is anyone's guess, although the initial signs do not inspire confidence.

Permit me then to conclude with this thought: At first glance the history of marriage and the family may appear to offer a wondrous array of diversity, but that first glance, like others, is more deceptive than trustworthy. For, on closer inspection, history teaches that civilization has always been accompanied by—indeed grounded in—an ideal of marriage and the family that attempts to join the biological difference of men and women in the common project of responsibility for the next generation.

6

The Legal Status of
Families as Institutions

Historically, our legal tradition has seen a fundamental contradiction between the family and the
individual, or, to put it differently, has preferred to treat
the family as a corporate unit rather than as a collection of isolated individuals. This preference accounted
for Blackstone's assertion,

> By marriage, the husband and wife are one person
> in law: that is, the very being or legal existence of
> the woman is suspended during the marriage, or
> at least is incorporated and consolidated into that
> of the husband: under whose wing, protection,
> and *cover,* she performs every thing. . . . Upon
> this principle, of an union of person in husband
> and wife, depend almost all the legal rights, du-

ties, and disabilities, that either of them acquire
by the marriage.[1]

By the same token, the children born into a family
were expected to fall under the authority of its head. The
family, in other words, was taken to constitute a unit
with a legal personality that transcended and subsumed
the individual rights of its constituent members.

The subordination of individual rights within the
family was never complete. Husbands were not legally
represented as owning their wives or their children—although they were known to sell one or the other. In principle, our tradition insisted upon a difference between
family members and slaves, although early advocates
of women's rights were wont to emphasize the similarity, arguing that married women, effectively, should be
viewed as slaves.[2] Instructively, Southern slaveholders
also evoked the similarities between family members
and slaves, not to protest the subordination of married
women, but to emphasize the humanity of slavery as a
social relation.[3]

The conjugal, or nuclear, family of our tradition has
always coexisted uneasily with notions of individual
rights and responsibilities, but until recently the heavy
hand of what Locke called "the Customs or Laws of the
Countrey"[4] obscured the full measure of the conflict. The
issue surfaced during the discussion of married women's
property rights in New York state during the mid-nine-

teenth century. Traditionalists opposed such rights on the ground that they would inevitably disrupt Blackstone's vision of the partners to a marriage as embodied in one person—the husband. Advocates of women's rights supported these rights on the ground that married women should indeed be recognized as separate persons—and be properly equipped to protect themselves against their husbands' possible abuse or malfeasance. In the event, reform of married women's property rights primarily resulted from the efforts of a third group, which sought not to further the independence of women, but rather to bring greater consistency to the law of property and to conform that law to the social and economic realities of the developing capitalist economy.[5]

The debates over the property rights of married women foreshadowed a continuing debate over the rights of women as individuals—that is, women's natural rights. Many of those who favored the persisting subordination of women within families did so because they favored a view of the family as an island of traditional hierarchy within a swirling sea of capitalism and individualism. It is, nonetheless, instructive to note that many of those who most staunchly supported the traditional concept of the family came to oppose the persistence of slavery, which many of them perceived as both a moral outrage and a fetter on economic development.

The issue might be seen as a difference over the appropriate composition of families. The emancipation of the slaves effectively ensured the triumph of a very narrow conception of family and, however unintentionally, paved the way for the recognition of the family as little more than a contractual union of free individuals. Intuitively, many of us would insist upon the distinction between wives and children, since the former first enter into the union voluntarily, whereas the latter are born into it and spend many years in a state of physical as well as economic dependence.[6] But our own times sadly reveal that the tensions between the freedom of individuals fundamental to the market and the family as a corporate unit also affect the status of children.

But questions remain. How should we think about the individual rights and responsibilities of family members? Does the family legally constitute something more than the sum of its constituent parts? To insist upon the family as a moral or social unit will not suffice without a clear—and implicitly corporate—legal status. The arguments against untoward (however untoward is defined) state interference in family affairs normally assume the existence of an intact family. I do not wish to engage such questions as whether parents who are Christian Scientists have the right to deny medical care to a child with leukemia or meningitis. Rather, I wish to raise the question of whether the arguments apply with equal force in cases of divorce or other forms of family disintegration. Are there legal grounds for denying an abused spouse or child recourse against the abuser? Do we not assume that family members have rights as individuals? And, if we do, what legal constraints do we place upon their independent relation to the polity and the market?

The point at issue is whether family members are held accountable for behaving towards other family members as they would be obligated to behave toward any other individual, or whether they are held accountable for behaving in certain ways toward other family members because of their special status as family members. Generally, this question has been framed as an inquiry into the power of fathers over other family members. Since the nineteenth century, and at an accelerating rate during the twentieth, the extreme forms of paternal power have come under increasing criticism and legal restriction. But the dismantling of that power has not led to new conceptions of the family as a corporate unit. Thus, the conception of the family as a group of individuals has followed naturally from the rejection of the view that the family's corporate identity was invested in the powers of its head. Tellingly, this rejection has also led to arguments that the concept and legal prerogatives of family relations should be extended to different groupings of individuals.

Until very recently, most people would have considered marital rape a contradiction in terms. If there is marriage, then there cannot be rape—although there may be an unacceptably violent exercise of marital rights. Today, many people assume that individual rights override marital rights—that behavior which is unacceptable if two people are not married is also unacceptable if they are married. The same could be said of child abuse. American society has always attributed some rights to members of families. Unlike early Roman society, we have never given fathers the right to kill their offspring with impunity. Even slaveholders were not legally allowed to kill their slaves on a whim.[7] But we have, at law, and especially in sentiment, granted special rights to the heads of households or families on the premise that their responsibility for family well-being entitled them to broad discretion in the exercise of their authority.

It is difficult, if not impossible, to separate the discussion of the family from the discussion of marriage. The movement for women's political and economic equality with men has primarily targeted women's traditional subordination within the family. In attempting to free women from that subordination, supporters of women's rights, have, however inadvertently, contributed to the destruction of the last vestiges of the family's corporate status. But opponents of women's rights and defenders of the family have failed no less woefully by not providing a new conception of the family as a corporate unit. Thus, discussions of women's and children's rights as members of family units invariably focus on what Elizabeth Wolgast has called "wrong rights"—their rights as autonomous individuals.[8] I would argue that a revitalized view of the family requires a new conception of its corporate identity. Such a conception must simultaneously allow for women's full participation as parents and for both parents' binding economic responsibility to their children.

If we are to defend the rights of families as units, then perhaps we should begin by endowing them with some greater measure of permanence and a more binding mutual responsibility than that granted by a normal contract. Perhaps parents should be denied the right to divorce until their children have attained their majority or are economically self-sufficient. In the case of intolerable unhappiness, a husband and wife could separate but would not be allowed to remarry or to assume economic responsibility for another family. In prerevolutionary France such a separation was known as the separation of bed and board.

To be sure, the enforcement of a married couple's binding economic responsibilities to each other and their children would require the cooperation of the federal government, but that is another debate. For the moment, permit me to conclude by reasserting that any serious discussion of families and individual responsibilities must begin with attention to the legal status of the family as an institution. A simple return to fathers of their historical power as heads of families will not suffice.

7

Historical Perspectives
on the Human Person

What is man that thou art mindful of him?
And the son of man that thou visitest him?
For thou has made him a little lower than the angels,
and thou has crowned him with glory and honour.

(Psalm 8:4–5)

Contemporary Western society—the most materi-
ally advanced in the history of the world—stands
alone and without precedent in the high value it attributes to the individual person. Simultaneously, it stands
exposed for the cheapness in which it holds human life.
Individual rights, human rights, self-esteem, and related
concepts dominate our culture's sense of the good that
must at all costs be defended. Yet unborn babies, terminally ill patients, or those who simply "dis" others in the
street are deemed expendable. Some lives embody the
essence of all that is admirable and worthy; others are to
be brushed aside as mere encumbrances. What remains

to be explained is who gets to decide which lives deserve respect and protection and which do not? Which of us has a right to decide which lives are worth living?

The well-known passage from the eighth psalm with which I began reminds us of the unique place the human person enjoys in creation, delicately poised between God, whom we are made to serve, and other living creatures—animals, fish, and birds—over whom God has granted us dominion. Contemporary culture, certainly in the United States and Europe, readily embraces the idea of man's dominion, but it shows markedly less enthusiasm for the idea that we rank lower in the hierarchy of merit than the angels and God. Our age has lost the psalmist's marvel at the unique blessings that God has showered upon us, preferring to assume that they are ours by right or by our own merit. Our complacency and self-satisfaction constitute the very essence of the culture of death against which Pope John Paul II warns us, for our boundless self-absorption blinds us to the value of others.

Caught in a dangerous paradox, our age simultaneously celebrates the unique value of human life and, however inadvertently, dismisses it as of no consequence. The life we are told to value is our own, and the more highly we value it the more easily we are tempted to discount the value of the lives of others. Preoccupation with the self at the expense of the other is nothing new: Cain established the model at the dawn of time. But our culture is breaking new ground in its attempt to establish selfishness as a higher principle, swathed in words like choice and fulfillment and autonomy.

In historical perspective, fixation upon the rights and unique value of the individual is something new. Until very recently, societies, including the most sophisticated societies of the Western world, have primarily regarded individual persons as members—and often as representatives—of groups, notably as members of families, but also of clans, tribes, social castes or estates, religious orders, or various trades or professions. The preferred forms of classification have varied, but the prevailing principle has held firm. A human person has been understood as someone's daughter, father, wife, or cousin—one link in a kinship that defines all of its members.

Christianity's insistence that God loves each individual broke radically with these patterns. Christianity affirmed the value of each particular person independent of ethnicity or sex or social standing, pronouncing, in the words of St. Paul. that "There is neither Jew nor Greek, there is neither bond nor free, there is neither male nor female: for ye are all one in Christ Jesus" (Galatians 3:28). More, in affirming the value of each, Christianity also affirmed the value of all. In other words, Christianity viewed the human person as both particular and embodied and as universal. The parable of the Good Samaritan was intended to teach Jesus' followers that the command to treat others with charity extended beyond the members of one's own ethnic group.

In Christian perspective, it was not possible truly to value any single person without valuing all persons or to value all persons (humanity) without valuing each single person. In both respects, Christianity broke with the tribalism of Ancient Israel and of much of the rest of the world, establishing new standards for the freedom each person should enjoy and for equality among persons. Christians did not, however, immediately attempt to impose their standards of spiritual dignity and spiritual equality upon relations among persons in the world. Over time, Christianity powerfully influenced the character of Western culture and even political life, but it owed much of its success to its remarkable ability to adapt to prevailing institutions and relations.

Only with the birth of modernism, notably in the dangerous—if widely celebrated—*cogito ergo sum* of René Descartes, did the disembedding of the individual person from the collectivity that grounded his identity begin to be viewed as a positive good. And only with the Enlightenment and the great eighteenth-century revolutions, notably the French Revolution of 1789, did the ideal of individual freedom attain preeminence over all forms of dependence and connection. In the waning years of the eighteenth century a political and intellectual vanguard proclaimed freedom the absolute antithesis of slavery and promulgated an understanding of freedom that favored the severing of all binding ties among human beings. Freedom in this lexicon means autonomy, self-determination, and independence from binding obligations, and this is the idea of freedom that has triumphed in our own time. Significantly, it originated as a radically secular idea, one frequently launched as a direct challenge to God. At the extreme, its consequences have been disastrous, but its most chilling implications may yet lie ahead. For it is the pursuit of this ideal of freedom which has brought us sexual liberation, abortion, assisted suicide, and an entire battery of assaults upon human life.

Before focusing upon the ways in which the radical pursuit of freedom has cheapened the value of the human person, however, it is necessary to acknowledge its many benefits. For the pursuit of human freedom has heightened the dignity and improved the lives of countless persons throughout the globe. The same history that has brought us the progressive discrediting of ties among persons has promoted a remarkable improvement in our understanding of the intrinsic value and dignity of each person. During recent centuries in many parts of the world, we have witnessed the abolition of slavery, an improvement in the position of women, greater attention to the discrete needs of children, respect for the needs and dignity of those who suffer from various handicaps, and so on. As Pope John Paul II has emphasized, these gains are not trivial, and on no account must we countenance their reversal. The puzzle remains that they have been accompanied by—and many would argue have depended upon—a hardening of attitudes towards the intrinsic value of all human persons and, especially, towards the binding ties among persons.

These two tendencies confront us with a paradox. On the one hand, we have a decreasing respect for the bonds among persons, and on the other an increasing commitment to the value and rights of previously oppressed groups of persons. On the one hand, we have an inflated concern for the rights and sensibilities of the individual, on the other a callous disregard for any life that in any way inconveniences us. This paradox challenges us to rethink our understanding of the human person, and especially the nature of the freedom and rights to which each of us is entitled. A misguided understanding of freedom will inescapably shape our understanding of the claims of life. Presumably, if one values human life, one opposes its willful termination, especially in its most vulnerable forms. Yet many of those who claim to value human life view abortion, assisted suicide, and even infanticide as necessary to its defense. For only the right to secure liberation from unwanted obligations protects the individual's freedom, which many view as the essence of any life worth living.

There is nothing surprising in the inclination to celebrate freedom as freedom from rather than freedom for, with the "from" understood as oppression and the "for" understood as service. Throughout history, the majority of labor has been unfree and the majority of women have been subordinated to men—initially their fathers or uncles and, later in life, their husbands or brothers. The Old Testament and classical literature both abound with examples. Agamemnon sacrificed his daughter, Iphigenia, to further his prospects for victory in the war against Troy. Until recent times, Hindus in India practiced suttee, whereby a widow was burned upon her husband's funeral pyre. Even in England, the sale of wives, although increasingly rare, persisted into the nineteenth century. Similarly, serfdom and slavery persisted throughout the world well into the nineteenth century and may still be found in some places today.

Under conditions in which even upper-class women rarely owned property in their own names and poor women might be beaten or bullied at will, it is not surprising that the early proponents of woman's rights embraced the analogy of slavery to describe their own condition and spoke of breaking the chains of their bondage. In practice, the women who were most likely to protest women's condition were from the urban middle class and sought to enjoy the same advantages of education and professional careers as their brothers. Such women normally benefited from codes of middle-class gentility and did not suffer from the horrors of abuse, sexual slavery, oppression, denigration, and desertion that plagued less privileged women—although some did. But they readily depicted their lot as indistinguishable from that of their less fortunate sisters. By the early twentieth century, the more radical were beginning to argue that marriage and childbearing were the true seedbeds of women's oppression, and to lobby for expanded legalization of divorce and artificial contraception.

Throughout these and related efforts, feminists continued to describe their goal as freedom from bondage and to claim their right to be regarded and treated as full human persons. Most people initially responded to the women's movement with hostility or incredulity, but few, even among opponents, claimed that women did not count as full human persons. They simply insisted that they were very different persons than men and, consequently, in need of a different social situation. The conviction that women and men, although both fully human persons, differed by nature persisted well into the twentieth century. Doctors argued that women's bodies made them unfit for college, psychologists argued that women had a distinct criminal disposition, lawyers argued that women should not be admitted to the bar, countless people argued that women should not vote, and virtually everyone assumed they should not engage in armed combat. Yet within the comparatively brief span of a century or so, feminists began to convince growing numbers of people of the justice of their cause, and, in so doing, to convince many that the natural differences between women and men had been vastly exaggerated.

We would be rash to minimize the magnitude of their extraordinary rhetorical victory, which significantly expanded the meaning of individual freedom and ultimately resulted in a reconfiguration of the moral landscape. By rhetorically extending the absolute opposition between freedom and slavery to the condition of women, feminists had declared any limitation upon a woman's freedom—including those imposed by her own body—as illegitimate. The campaigns against slavery and the subordination of women both embodied a worthy—indeed necessary—commitment to increasing the dignity accorded to all human persons and the equality among them. Both, in other words, represented what we may reasonably view as moral progress. Yet both tacitly embraced the flawed premise that to be authentic, freedom must be unlimited, or better, unconditional, which, by a sleight of hand, reduced the ties among persons to another form of bondage.

Throughout the modern period, material change has undergirded and, arguably, accelerated changing attitudes towards the human person. Modern urban societies provide many more possibilities than traditional rural societies for people to live alone. In rural society the interdependence of persons constitutes the very fabric of life, and none can survive without mutual cooperation. Typically, rural societies also favor a clear articulation of authority whereby one member of the family or group assumes primary responsibility for and direction of the rest. Typically, that person has been the male head of a household, family, or tribe. What modern critics are loath to understand is that rarely—if ever—could such a head exercise his authority without the tacit or active collaboration of those over whom he presides.

We should, nonetheless, err in romanticizing traditional societies, although many find it tempting to do so. These were worlds in which life for many could often be "nasty, brutish, and short." They were worlds in which cruelty among persons abounded and in which death stalked young and old alike. Not for nothing did the Palestine of Jesus' time abound with cripples and lepers, hemorrhaging women and desperately ill children. Population has increased in the modern world because modern medicine has done so much to control disease and defer death, more than because of an increase in the number of births. The prevalence of disease and the likelihood of early death have led many traditional rural societies to value highly women's fertility and the birth of children. Here too, however, romanticization misleads, for even groups that welcome births might turn around and kill infants they could not support. Traditional societies, even when Christian, did not necessarily manifest "respect for life" in the sense we use the phrase today. They did, however, know that their agricultural and military survival depended upon sustaining their population or increasing it.

These traditional rural worlds did not ordinarily celebrate the unique attributes of each person as we are wont to do today, but they did value each person as an essential member of the family, household, or community. No family could function for long without a mother or appropriate female substitute, typically a maiden aunt, and widowers with small children were normally quick to remarry. Similarly, it could not function for long without a strong senior male who, with or without assistance, could bring in crops, care for livestock, and defend against predators. Personal autonomy did not figure as the *summum bonum* among rural folk for whom interdependence provided the best guarantee of family or community survival. Modern critics of those bonds frequently focus upon the injustice of specific forms of subordination: slave to master, wife to husband, children to parents. But in repudiating the injustice of women's subordination to men, for example, they end by attacking all binding ties as obstacles to women's liberation, not just specific abuses, which cry out for uncompromising repudiation. The reasoning seems to be that binding ties have always disadvantaged women and that abuse is the rule rather than the exception.

The acceleration of economic progress transformed the rural world, mainly by moving the economic center of gravity to cities, which offered new possibilities for people to live in smaller groups or even on their own. Drawing ever larger numbers of people into wage labor, capitalism insinuated itself into the interstices of families and households, reinforcing the culture's growing tendency to encourage members to see themselves as individuals. Capitalism's dependence upon an accelerating consumption of material goods furthered the cultural emphasis upon the psychological goods of autonomy, satisfaction of desire, and instant gratification. Secular psychology contributed mightily to the transformation of "I want" from evidence of selfishness or greed to a sign of mental health. In the same spirit, it declared war on the idea of sin, which it denounced as nothing more than a sadistic campaign to thwart people's enjoyment of life. Multinational corporations have powerfully supported and indeed advanced these tendencies, for their interests do not benefit from stable families, but rather from a large pool of unencumbered employees, who are prepared to live with their cell phones always turned on and a suitcase always packed.

Some modern scholars have delighted in exposing the ways in which traditional societies held persons in thrall to repressive norms, primarily fostered by punitive, misogynist, patriarchal, and hierarchical forms of Christianity—especially Catholicism. Others have tended to romanticize folk and working-class cultures, presenting them as more spontaneous and less repressed than the middle-class culture of the modern urban world. Both views contain a measure of truth and a measure of falsehood. But both, however inadvertently, suggest a greater emphasis upon the bonds among persons than commonly prevails today. Whether one views the traditional world as good or bad—or, more plausibly, a mixture of both—it was a world in which people developed a sense of themselves as persons as a function of their relations with others, often beginning with their relation to God. Nor were these attitudes unique to Christians. In different versions, they prevailed among Jews, Muslims, Hindus, and Confucians, as well as among adherents to various forms of polytheism, animism, and other systems of belief.

Here, I do not wish to engage in debates about the deeper character of the various faiths but simply to underscore that all have shared a sense that the individual could only prosper in union with the group. These were faiths that viewed the human person as an integral part of a larger group whose needs would take precedence over the specific person's whims and desires—faiths that promoted unambiguous messages about good and bad, that attributed little importance to individual subjectivity, and that had little interest in progress. Like all others, traditional oral cultures do change, but as they lack written records, they do not register change but rather absorb it into "the way things have always been." Modern secular cultures, in sharp contrast, focus upon the dynamism of change and the superiority of the "new."

Traditional societies' conservatism with respect to the rights and independence of the individual, like their strong commitment to holding persons to prescribed social and familial roles, represented above all a commitment to the survival and internal coherence of the family or community. In this spirit, they rejected individual judgment as an appropriate guide for behavior, not least because they fully recognized the disruptive power of individual passions, notably anger and desire. Saint Paul said it clearly in his Letter to the Galatians (5:13–15): "For you have been called to liberty, brethren; only do not use liberty as an occasion for sensuality, but by charity serve one another. For the whole law is fulfilled in one word: Thou shalt love they neighbor as thyself. But if you bite and devour one another, take heed or you will be consumed by one another." Mindful of the dangers of strife within families and among neighbors, traditional societies might enforce their convictions through methods that seem repressive or even brutal today. Even the more rigid, however, did not often rely upon the extreme measures that some contemporary groups have been known to use, such as killing girls who try to attend school. Today's extremes, as Bernard Lewis, the great authority on Islam, has argued, primarily embody a panicky reaction against what are perceived as the excesses of the disintegration and decadence of contemporary Western society.

Those who fear the destructive potential of Western cultures do not err. It is child's play to muster examples of rampant consumerism and what Karl Marx called the fetishism of commodities, which today seems to be degenerating into the commodification of personal relations. Even the most casual acquaintance with American media—especially television—reveals a world that has all but dehumanized persons by severing the binding connections among them. For all the talk of the warmth and support of substitute, alternate, or proxy families, American culture depicts a world in which family represents no more than a person's current choice, which may easily be replaced by another choice. We have never lacked for critics of the symptoms of this culture of easy-come, easy-go, and recent years may even have seen an increase in defenses of marriage, attacks upon the harm that divorce wreaks upon children, and defenses of the value of modesty and premarital chastity. We have dedicated groups and individuals who oppose abortion and so-called assisted suicide, and we are apparently seeing an appreciable increase in the number of Americans who have doubts about the desirability of legal abortion, especially after the first trimester. What we lack—and the lack is devastating—is an insistent, concerted counteroffensive. We lack it because more often than not even those who oppose many specific forms of social decomposition accept the main premise that underlies them all, namely the primacy of the convenience and comfort of the individual.

Recently, I had the opportunity to speak with a group of faithful Catholic women, many of whom attend daily Mass, all of whom rightly consider themselves devout. Blessed with considerable material comfort, they have all given generously to the parish for decades, and would all consider themselves loyal supporters of the church. During my talk, I mentioned my growing horror at abortion as one of the important elements in my own conversion to Catholicism. When we broke into informal conversation over lunch, one of the women drew me aside because she wanted me to know that notwithstanding her respect for the teachings of the Magisterium, if she had a thirteen-year-old daughter who was impregnated during a rape, she would whisk her off to an abortionist before you could say "boo." Startled, I responded, "And what if she were twenty-three and finishing law school?" She looked startled and suddenly abashed.

An intelligent woman, my acquaintance readily understood my point that, with each passing day, we Catholics seem to be finding it easier to acquiesce in the logic of the secular world. The results are disastrous for our understanding of the human person and our ability to sustain binding relations with others. We have too readily acquiesced in the secular view of the human person as, above all, an individual who is fundamentally disconnected from other individuals. The disconnected individual may enter into relations with others, but the relations remain contractual, subject to termination at the choice of either party. Such instrumental relations are bad enough for adults, but they are disastrous for children, not to mention the handicapped, the unborn, and the terminally ill. More, they are in direct contradiction to the teachings and spirit of our faith. For how are we to understand Jesus' repeated commands that we love one another as ourselves, if not as a command to recognize that our own personhood depends upon our recognition of the other. In this sense, the modern era has not merely transformed the idea of the person, it has effectively abandoned it in favor of the subjective individual.

The irony of our situation is painful. In historical perspective, we appear to place a higher value on the individual—as an individual—than any previous society, yet we increasingly view the individual as essentially a subjective being whose will and desires should determine what he or she is due. Only in this spirit would it be so easy to present an unborn baby—and, for some people, one that has been born as well—as nothing more than an obstacle to its mother's freedom to pursue the goals she has chosen. Rather than emphasizing the mother's obligation to the human life she is carrying, our culture increasingly insists upon her right to be free of it. The mother's right to choose thus negates the unborn child's right to live, and by claiming this right to deny the personhood of another, the mother negates her own. No longer a person whose being, sense of self, and place in the world depend upon her relations with others, beginning with her primary relation with God, the woman becomes an isolated individual, disconnected from others whom she can see only as objects to be manipulated or obstacles to be cleared away.

Christianity led the way in promoting a view of each person as valuable, unique, beloved, and endowed with freedom. Yet Christianity also presupposed that each person derived meaning from relations with others—that the very essence of personhood lay in the recognition of the equal personhood of the other. Thus, the Christian ideals of the value and freedom of each individual co-existed comfortably with a culture that placed a much higher value on the group than the individual, who was primarily understood as a member of the group. The Reformation placed a new emphasis on the individual, but Luther, Calvin, and their heirs remained tied to a communal ethos. Their doctrine of *sola scriptura*, however, opened the way for a disastrous slide into a rising secular bourgeois individualism that, in our time, has largely overwhelmed the protestant Churches and—let us admit frankly—is now threatening our own. For as individualism gradually triumphed over the collective values of traditional culture, it did so in radically secular terms and usually in direct rebellion against the church.

This history has left us a dangerous and insidious legacy, for the individualism that spearheaded a broad cultural revolt against the teachings of the church also insinuated itself into the thinking of Christians, including Catholics. The goods that individualism purported to offer are almost irresistibly seductive: tolerance of the behavior of others; delight in bodies and sexuality; acceptance of oneself, complete with flaws; the legitimacy of desire; and on and on. Consequently, any attempt to oppose or criticize them seems ungenerous, judgmental, and intolerant. Who am I to tell another how to live his or her life? What gives me the right to impose punitive values upon another?

In *Writings on an Ethical Life*, Peter Singer reaffirms his argument that "the life of a fetus . . . is of no greater value than the life of a non-human animal at a similar level of rationality, self consciousness, awareness, capacity to feel, etc., and that since no fetus is a person, no fetus has the same claim to life as a person." This reasoning, Singer continues, necessarily applies "to the newborn baby as much as to the fetus." Thus, if we but free ourselves from the "emotionally moving but strictly irrelevant aspects of the killing of a baby, we can see that the grounds for not killing persons do not apply to newborn infants."[1]

Singer's chilling perspective exposes the ultimate logic of the emphasis upon the individual's right to choose, for in Singer's world, the individual may first decide what counts as life before deciding between life and death. By this sinister logic, the choices of rational individuals may never be judged evil, for they are always choosing life as they define it. Thus does our purported and seductive solicitude for the freedom of each individual mask the ominous tendency in our Western societies to objectify the very individuals we pretend to celebrate. Substituting rights for mutual bonds, we are substituting the individual for the human person, thereby freeing ourselves to deny the humanity of others. Thus does the slaughter of the innocents become "a woman's right to choose."

8

The Family and Pope John Paul II

Not long since, most people took the concept of family for granted, even when they did not necessarily take it to signify the same set of human relations. Today, however, the family ranks as one of the most hotly contested of concepts, and debates about its nature and function evoke heated passions in all quarters. The very existence of the debates points to far-reaching and portentous changes in the most fundamental understandings of the human condition, notably the relations between the individual and the community; the claims of sexuality and desire; the proper understanding of women's nature and vocation; the relationship between men and women, and the mutual relations and responsibilities of parents and children.

No one was more conscious of and attentive to the possible implications of these changes than Pope John Paul II. From the early days of his pastorate in Poland until his later reflections upon the challenges of the new millennium, he urged Catholics to understand the family as the necessary grounding and context for the human person.

This concern for the family as the fundamental custodian of life amid an encroaching Culture of Death always figured at the center of Pope John Paul II's theology, philosophy, psychology, anthropology and social teaching. Commitment to the strengthening of families in a world that tends to tear them apart always ranked high among his sense of pastoral responsibilities. As papal biographers have noted, conditions in the Poland of Karol Wojtyla's youth, young manhood, and early clerical career continuously reminded him of the importance of the family both as a protection against the onslaughts of Nazism and communism, and as the core building block of any decent and humane—any truly Christian—society. In this respect, the pope's dedication to the ideal and the practical reality of family constituted a foundational element of his understanding of the meaning and mission of Catholicism during the closing decades of the second millennium and the beginning of the third.

As an archbishop and an active participant in the Second Vatican Council, he played a major role in the drafting of *Gaudium et Spes* (Pastoral Constitution on the Church in the Modern World). *Gaudium et Spes* (GS) emphasizes the ways in which the modern world offers man unprecedented opportunities and unprecedented dangers—new forms of freedom and new forms of slavery. With the dramatic triumph of industrial life over rural life, "the human race has passed from a rather static concept of reality to a more dynamic, evolutionary one," and this transition has confronted us with a daunting array of new problems—problems that must ultimately be understood as a crisis of humanism (GS, 5).

Emphasizing the importance of marriage and family as the bedrock for people who attempt to respond to this crisis, the document also acknowledges that the "excellence" of marriage as an institution "is not everywhere reflected with equal brilliance, since polygamy, the plague of divorce, so-called free love, and other disfigurements all have an obscuring effect" (GS, 47). Marriage and the family have suffered innumerable pressures and have often—some would claim more often than not—failed to realize their highest mission.

Nothing in John Paul II's writings, before or after his ascension to the papacy, suggests that he was naïve about the multiple variations in marriage and family throughout the history of the world. He nonetheless insisted, with *Gaudium et Spes*, that the "intimate partnership of married life and love has been established by the Creator and qualified by his laws and is rooted in the conjugal covenant of irrevocable personal consent." Thus, he leaves no excuse for misunderstanding: "God himself is the author of matrimony, endowed as it is with various benefits and purposes" (GS, 48).

From Wojtyla's early years as a priest, he had an immediate grasp of the social and political forces that threatened the solidity of marriages and family life. Initially, he recognized the threat in the Communist intervention into family life, and especially the Communists' hostility to the sacramental character of marriage. Subsequently, however, he became increasingly sensitive to the ways in which the wealth some nations have and the globalization of the economy threatened the integrity of marriage and family life.

In different ways and at different rates, both secularism and fundamentalism have contributed to what Pope John Paul II designated the Culture of Death—a culture that holds human life cheaper and cheaper until it drains it of all intrinsic value, a culture that transforms people into objects or even obstacles. This is not a self-portrait that appeals to the affluent denizens of the developed world, who reject the very notion of the Culture of Death, and even more the view of themselves as its purveyors. Caught up in a world overflowing with commodities and armed with a science that promises to extend and create every human life, they find it easy to take their unprecedented material prosperity as the standard for human fulfillment. Nor do the prophets of traditional religion view themselves as reactionary and ignorant.

Throughout the globe, multinational corporations are drawing people out of traditional families and communities, binding some individuals to the prospects of new possibilities, while condemning their kin to the dustbins of the cities or the dust bowls of the villages. The greatest—and most awesome—power of the global economy lies in its ability to touch everything. In this respect, it acts as the ultimate solvent of the bonds that shape and guarantee our humanity—our intrinsic worth and dignity as persons. The formidable challenge of our times, as John Paul II demonstrably understood, lies in the defense, reconstitution, and adaptation of these bonds to conform to the valuable aspects of globalization, without succumbing to its destructive tendencies.

The twentieth century included significant changes in the status and opportunities of women, and most of them were long overdue. Nowhere is it written that men and women's specific natures entitle men to beat, enslave, exploit, or otherwise abuse women. Our understanding of women's talents and capabilities changed radically during the past century, as has our understanding of the employments for which women are suited. Today, however, we confront a dangerous polarization that pits traditionalists, who condemn all change in women's situation, against radicals, who insist that the very notion of a distinct female nature is a repressive fiction. The worst consequence of this confrontation is that it has drowned out the voices of those who regard most of the changes in women's situation as beneficial, while continuing to accept the significance of women's embodied being, with its unique capacity to bear and nurture new life.

Feminists rage at the pope's claims that "women's singular relationship with human life derives from her vocation to motherhood"; that "the maternal mission is also the basis of particular responsibility"; or that "the woman is called to offer the best of herself to the baby growing within her," since "it is precisely by making herself 'gift' that she comes to know herself better and is fulfilled in her femininity" (*Angelus* message, July 19, 1995).

Many deplore his insistence that women's employment must always respect the "fundamental duty" of the "most delicate tasks of motherhood" (*Angelus* message, July 23, 1995). Most do not like the notion that women's rights include any binding duties at all. Rejecting the pope's vision of the responsibilities that accompany women's rights, feminists promote an unrestricted freedom that disconcertingly resembles equal membership in the Culture of Death.

The crux of the difference between the feminists and the late pope lies in their respective understandings of women's nature and mission. Feminists dismiss injunctions to service, binding obligations, and loving self-sacrifice as so many hypocritical pieties designed to perpetuate women's subordination to men. The pope, in contrast, viewed them as fundamental Christian precepts that require the compliance of men as well as women.

The experience of recent years has blindingly exposed the agonizing difficulty of attempts to combine responsibility to a family, especially children, with a professional fast track, or even with full-time employment. The pope effectively argued that wives and mothers have a moral obligation to put their families first. Feminists argue that women have no greater obligation to do so than men. Unfortunately, when parents struggle over who should be freer to do less, the children get less and less—with ominous consequences for the human and moral fabric of society as a whole.

Normally, few would fault the pope's quiet insistence that the abundance of love and peace in the world ultimately depends upon the personal education each child receives in the family. Such education, however, depends upon service—the service of parents, frequently mothers to children—and upon willingness to forgo or postpone acquisition of the signs of status most valued by the world.

The pope's recurring demand that the world accommodate women's needs as wives, mothers and workers, like his insistence upon women's rights to equal dignity and opportunity, testified to his understanding of the difficulties and the pain. But he insisted that, to surmount these conflicts, women must cultivate the peace of heart that frees them to be teachers of peace: "Inner peace comes from knowing that one is loved by God and from the desire to respond to his love," he said in his message for the 1995 World Day of Peace.

For Christians this injunction applies as much to men as to women, but Christian teaching has traditionally held that it applies to them differently. John Paul II sought to reaffirm the difference while he combats the oppressive and exploitative uses to which it has been put. In a corrupt world, his admirable vision remains elusive and formidably difficult to realize. Women will understandably continue to wonder how much they can afford to sacrifice without the assurance of support for themselves and their children. These legitimate worries admit of no easy answers, but, in facing the risks, we might profitably reflect upon the pope's essential message: namely, that the rising tide of the Culture of Death will not be stayed until individuals, one by one, begin to repudiate its claims upon their souls.

Afterword: A Well-Lived Life

Robert P. George

Elizabeth Fox-Genovese was a scholar as notable for her bravery as for her brilliance. After what she described as her "long apprenticeship" in the world of secular liberal intellectuals, it was careful reflection on the central moral questions of our time that led her first to doubt and then to abandon both liberalism and secularism. Needless to say, this did not endear her to her former allies.

At the heart of her doubts about secular liberalism (and what she described as "radical, upscale feminism") was its embrace of abortion and its (continuing) dalliance with euthanasia. At first, she went along with abortion, albeit reluctantly, believing that women's rights to develop their talents and control their destinies required its legal availability. But Betsey (as she was known by her friends) was not one who could avert her eyes from inconvenient facts. The central fact about abortion is that it is the deliberate killing of a developing child in the womb. For Betsey, euphemisms such as "products of conception," "termination of pregnancy," "privacy," and "choice" ultimately could not hide that fact. She came to see that to countenance abortion is not to respect women's "privacy" or liberty; it is to suppose that some people have the right to decide whether others will live or die. In a statement that she knew would enflame many on the left and even cost her valued friendships, she declared that "no amount of past oppression can justify women's oppression of the most vulnerable among us."

Betsey knew that public pro-life advocacy would be regarded by many in the intellectual establishment as intolerable apostasy—especially from one of the founding mothers of "women's studies." She could have been forgiven for keeping mum on the issue and carrying on with her professional work on the history of the American South. But keeping mum about fundamental matters of right and wrong was not in her character. And though she valued her standing in the intellectual world, she cared for truth and justice more. And so she spoke out ever more passionately in defense of the unborn.

And the more she thought and wrote about abortion and other life issues, the more persuaded she became that the entire secular liberal project was misguided. Secular liberals were not deviating from their principles in endorsing killing, whether by abortion or euthanasia, in the name of individual "choice"; they were following them to their logical conclusions. But this revealed a profound contradiction at the heart of secular liberal ideology, for the right of some individuals to kill others undermines any ground of principle on which an idea of individual rights or dignity can be founded.

Even in her early life as a secular liberal, she was never among those who disdained religious believers or held them in contempt. As a historian and social critic, she admired the cultural and moral achievements of Judaism and Christianity. As her doubts about secularism grew, she began to consider seriously whether religious claims might actually be true. Reason led her to the door of faith, and prayer enabled her to walk through it. As she herself described her conversion from secularism to Catholicism, it had a large intellectual component; yet it was, in the end, less her choice than God's grace.

Betsey continued her scholarly labors, especially in collaboration with her husband Eugene Genovese, our nation's most distinguished historian of American slavery. Not long ago, Cambridge University Press published their masterwork, *The Mind of the Master Class*. Soon after Betsey's own religious conversion, Gene (who had long been an avowed Marxist, but who had gradually moved in the direction of cultural and political conservatism) returned to the Catholic faith of his boyhood under the influence of his beloved wife.

As if she had not already antagonized the intellectual establishment enough, Betsey soon began speaking out in defense of marriage and sexual morality. Her root-and-branch rejection of the ideology of the sexual revolution—an ideology that now enjoys the status of infallible dogma among many secular liberal intellectuals—was based on a profound appreciation of the centrality of marriage to the fulfillment of men and women as sexually complementary spouses; to the well-being of children, for whom the love of mother and father for each other and for them is literally indispensable; and to society as a whole, which depends on the marriage-based family for the rearing of responsible and upright citizens. If her pro-life advocacy angered many liberal intellectuals, her outspoken defense of marriage and traditional norms of sexual morality made them apoplectic.

Betsey's marriage to Gene was one of the great love stories of our time. They were two very different personalities, perfectly united. He was the head of the family; she was in charge of everything. Their affection for each other created a kind of force field into which friends were drawn in love for both of them. Although unable to have children of their own, they lavished parental care and concern on their students and younger colleagues, who in turn worshipped them.

Betsey leaves us many fine works of historical scholarship and social criticism—works admired by honest scholars across the political spectrum. Even more importantly, her life provides an unsurpassed example of intellectual integrity and moral courage. Her fervent witness to the sanctity of human life and the dignity of marriage and the family will continue to inspire.

A Short List of
Good Books on Marriage

Dawn Eden. *The Thrill of the Chaste: How to Find Fulfill-ment While Keeping Your Clothes On*. Nashville, TN: Thomas Nelson, 2006.

Peter J. Elliott. *What God Has Joined: The Sacramental-ity of Marriage*. New York: Alba House, 1990.

Robert P. George and Jean Bethke Elshtain, eds. *The Meaning of Marriage: Family, State, Market, and Mor-als*. Dallas: Spence Publishing, 2006.

Mary Ann Glendon. *Abortion and Divorce in Western Law: American Failures, European Challenges*. Cam-bridge, MA: Harvard University Press, 1987.

Gail Godwin. *The Good Husband* [novel]. New York: Ballantine Books, 1994.

John Paul II. *Love and Responsibility*. San Francisco: Ignatius Press, 1993 [1960].

Amy A. Kass and Leon R. Kass, eds. *Wing to Wing, Oar to Oar: Readings on Courtship and Marriage*. Notre Dame, IN: University of Notre Dame Press, 2000.

Christopher Lasch. *Women and the Common Life: Love, Marriage, and Feminism*, edited by Elisabeth Lasch-Quinn. New York: W. W. Norton & Co., 1997.

Elizabeth Marquardt. *Between Two Worlds: The Inner Lives of Children of Divorce*. New York: Crown Publishers, 2005.

Jennifer Roback Morse. *Smart Sex: Finding Life-Long Love in a Hook-Up World*. Dallas: Spence Publishing, 2005.

Linda J. Waite and Maggie Gallagher. *The Case for Marriage: Why Married People Are Happier, Healthier, and Better Off Financially*. New York: Broadway Books, 2000.

Judith S. Wallerstein, Julia M. Lewis, and Sandra Blakeslee. *The Unexpected Legacy of Divorce: The 25-Year Landmark Study*. New York: Hyperion, 2000.

Barbara Dafoe Whitehead. *The Divorce Culture: Rethinking Our Commitments to Marriage and Family.* New York: Vintage, 1998.

W. Bradford Wilcox. *Soft Patriarchs, New Men: How Christianity Shapes Fathers and Husbands.* Chicago: University of Chicago Press, 2004.

James Q. Wilson. *The Marriage Problem: How Our Culture Has Weakened Families.* New York: HarperCollins, 2002.

John Witte Jr. *From Sacrament to Contract: Marriage, Religion, and Law in the Western Tradition.* Louisville, KY: Westminster John Knox Press, 1997.

Notes

Introduction

1. Video footage of these lectures, including the question-and-answer periods, is available online at http://web.princeton.edu/sites/jmadison/calendar/videos.html.
2. Personal correspondence to friends, June 30, 2003.
3. Elizabeth Fox-Genovese, "The Web of Grace," *Crisis* (November 1997), 48.
4. Ibid., 46.
5. Ibid., 44.
6. Robert P. George, "Women We Love: In Praise of a Few Ladies," *National Review On-Line* (February 14, 2006).
7. Fox-Genovese, "The Web of Grace," 46.
8. Ibid., 44.
9. Gail Godwin, *Evensong* (New York: Ballantine Books, 1999), 32.
10. Karol Wojtyla, *Love and Responsibility* (San Francisco: Ignatius Press, 1993), 139.

Chapter 1: Male and Female He Created Them

1. See Fay Yarbrough's dissertation, "'those Disgracefull and unnatural Matches': Interracial Sex and Cherokee Society in the Nineteenth Century," Emory University, 2003. Yarbrough's *Race and the Cherokee Nation: Sovereignty in the Nineteenth Century* (Philadelphia: University of Pennsylvania Press, 2007) continues this research.

2. Colin Morris, *The Discovery of the Individual, 1050–1200* (Toronto: University of Toronto Press, 1987).

3. From Georges Bizet's *Carmen* (1875): "Si tu ne m'aimes pas je t'aime. Et si je t'aime, prends gard à toi."

4. On Richard Wagner's influence and the theme of *liebestod*, see Laura Maricque Barlament's dissertation, "Wagner's Tristan and the Limits of Love: Tristanism in Thomas Mann, Kate Chopin, and Willa Cather," Emory University, 2001.

5. Georg Friedrich Hegel, *The Philosophy of Right*.

Chapter 2: Different or Equal?
The Compromise of Separate Spheres

1. Carolyn Heilbrun, *Writing a Woman's Life* (New York: W. W. Norton & Company, 1988; repr., New York: Ballantine Books, 1989), 77.

2. Rachel Blau DuPlessis, *Writing Beyond the Ending: Narrative Strategies of Twentieth-Century Women Writers* (Bloomington, IN: Indiana University Press, 1985), 1.

3. Adam Smith, "Domestic Law," from *Lectures on Jurisprudence*, Volume 5, paragraph 773, of Glasgow Edition of the *Works and Correspondences of Adam Smith*, ed. R. L. Meek, D. D. Raphael, and P. G. Stein (reprint, Indianapolis: Liberty Fund, 1982).

4. Christopher Lasch, *Haven in a Heartless World: The Family Besieged* (New York: Basic Books, 1977; reprint, New York: W. W. Norton & Company, 1995).

5. Sir William Blackstone, *Commentaries on the Laws of England* (1765–1769).

6. Austen began writing most of her novels around 1797, although none was published until about fifteen years later, when the major ones began to appear in quick succession.
7. Thomas Hobbes, *Leviathan* (1651).
8. Orlando Patterson, *Slavery and Social Death: A Comparative Study* (Cambridge, MA: Harvard University Press, 1982).

Chapter 3: Marriage on Trial

1. See also Alan Charles Raul, "Undermining Society's Morals," *Washington Post* (November 28, 2003), and Robert P. George, "One Man, One Woman: The Case for Preserving the Definition of Marriage," *Wall Street Journal* (November 28, 2003).
2. James Q. Wilson, *The Marriage Problem: How Our Culture Has Weakened Families* (New York: HarperCollins, 2003), 176.

Chapter 4: Women and the Family

1. Nadya Labi, "The Hunter and the Choirboy," *Time* 151, no. 13 (April 6, 1998).
2. Survey conducted by the Higher Education Research Institute at the University of California, reported on by Leo Reisberg, *Chronicle of Higher Education* (January 25, 1999).
3. Princeton Survey Research Associates, "The Impact of Religious Organizations on Gender Equality: A Report of Findings from a National Survey of Women" (January 7, 1999).
4. James Davison Hunter, *Before the Shooting Begins: Searching for Democracy as the Culture Wars Rage* (New York: Free Press, 1994). See also Elizabeth Fox-Genovese's review of *Before the Shooting Begins* in *First Things* (June/July 1994).
5. For a fuller development of this argument, see Elizabeth Fox-Genovese's "A Conversion Story" in *First Things* (April 2000).
6. Aristotle said different "in kind"; Locke said "distinct." See Tiffany R. Jones and Larry Peterman, "Whither the Family and Family Privacy?" paper delivered at the annual meeting of the American Political Science Association, Boston, Mas-

sachusetts, September 1998, for a discussion of these traditions and developments. The tradition in political theory stretches from Aristotle to John Locke and beyond.

7. For an extended discussion of these issues, see Elizabeth Fox-Genovese's *Feminism without Illusions: A Critique of Individualism* (Chapel Hill, NC: University of North Carolina Press, 1991); and *"Feminism Is Not the Story of My Life": How Today's Feminist Elite Has Lost Touch with the Real Concerns of Women* (New York: Doubleday, 1996).

8. Jones and Peterman, "Whither the Family?" referring to the view of June Aline Eichbaum, "Towards an Autonomy-Based Theory of Constitutional Privacy: Beyond the Ideology of Familial Privacy," 14 *Harvard Civil Rights and Civil Liberties Law Review* 364 (1979): 381–82; and Anita Allen, *Uneasy Access: Privacy for Women in a Free Society* (Lanham, MD: Rowman & Littlefield, 1988), 84–85.

9. Arlie Hochschild with Anne Machung, *The Second Shift* (New York: Viking, 1989).

10. Mary Ann Glendon, *Rights Talk: The Impoverishment of Political Discourse* (New York: Free Press, 1991).

11. 428 U.S. 52(1976), at 70, cited by Jones and Peterman, "Whither the Family?"

12. Ibid.

13. *Planned Parenthood of Southeastern Pennsylvania v Casey*, 112 Sup. Ct. 2791 (1992).

14. Steven Nock, *Marriage in Men's Lives* (New York: Oxford University Press, 1998).

15. Andrew Cherlin, *Marriage, Divorce, Remarriage*, rev. ed. (Cambridge, MA: Harvard University Press, 1992); and Larry L. Bumpass and James A. Sweet, "Cohabitation, Marriage and Union Stability: Preliminary Findings from NSFH2," NSFH Working Paper, no. 65 (University of Wisconsin–Madison: Center for Demography and Ecology, 1995).

16. Eleanor E. Macoby, *The Two Sexes* (Cambridge, MA: Harvard University Press, 1998).

17. George A. Akerlof, Janet L. Yellen, and Michael L. Katz, "An Analysis of Out-of-Wedlock Childbearing in the United States," *Quarterly Journal of Economics* 111 (1996): 277–317. It

should be noted the Akerlof, Yellen, and Katz write from the liberal rather than the conservative end of the political spectrum. Indeed, President Clinton appointed Janet L. Yellen to the Council of Economic Advisors.

18. George A. Akerlof, "Men Without Children," *Economic Journal* 108 (1998): 287–309.

19. Sara McLanahan and Gary Sandfur, *Growing Up with a Single Parent: What Hurts, What Helps* (Cambridge, MA: Harvard University Press, 1994), 1.

20. Cynthia C. Harper and Sara S. McLanahan, "Father Absence and Youth Incarceration," paper delivered at the annual meeting of the American Sociological Association, San Francisco, 1998; David Popenoe, *Life without Father: Compelling New Evidence That Fatherhood and Marriage Are Indispensable for the Good of Children and Society* (New York: Free Press, 1996); Nicholas Zill and Charlotte A. Schoenborn, "Developmental Learning and Emotional Problems: Health of Our Nation's Children, United States, 1988," Advance Data, National Center for Health Statistics, no. 120, 9.

21. Andrew Hacker, "The War over the Family," *New York Review of Books* 44, no. 19 (December 4, 1997): 36–37.

22. For a fuller discussion of these trends, see Fox-Genovese, "Feminism Is Not the Story of My Life." See also Francis Fukuyama, *The Great Disruption: Human Nature and the Disruption of Social Order* (New York: Free Press, 1999).

23. Bumpass and Sweet, "Cohabitation, Marriage, and Union Stability"; and Christopher Ellison, John Bartkowski, and Kristin Anderson, "Are there Religious Variations in Domestic Violence?" *Journal of Family Issues* 20 (1999): 87–113.

24. Danielle Crittenden, *What Our Mothers Didn't Tell Us: Why Happiness Eludes the Modern Woman* (New York, Simon & Schuster, 1999), 110.

25. For the sexual and economic revolution, see Fox-Genovese, "Feminism Is Not the Story of My Life." See also Fukuyama, *The Great Disruption*; the discussions in Alan Wolfe, "The Shock of Old," *New Republic* 4411 (August 2, 1999): 42–46; and David Brooks, "Disruption and Redemption," *Policy Review* 95 (June/July, 1999): 72–77.

26. Wilfred M. McClay, *The Masterless: Self and Society in Modern America* (Chapel Hill, NC: University of North Carolina Press, 1994).
27. Orlando Patterson, *Freedom in the Making of Western Culture* (New York: Basic Books, 1991).
28. Mary Stewart Von Leeuwen, "Re-Inventing the Ties That Bind: Feminism and the Family at the Close of the Twentieth Century," in *Religion Feminism and the Family*, ed. Anne Carr and Mary Stewart Von Leeuwen (Louisville, KY: Westminster John Knox, 1996). See also Mary Stewart Von Leeuwen, et al. *After Eden: Facing the Challenge of Gender Reconciliation* (Grand Rapids, MI: Eerdmans, 1993).
29. Gail Goodwin, *The Good Husband* (New York: Ballantine Books, 1994), 465.

Chapter 5: Thoughts on the History of the Family

1. Philippe Ariès, *Centuries of Childhood: A Social History of Family Life*, trans. Robert Baldick (New York: Alfred Knopf, 1962).
2. Lawrence Stone, *The Family, Sex, and Marriage in England, 1500–1800* (New York: Harper & Row, 1977).
3. See, for example, Randolph Trumbach, *The Rise of the Egalitarian Family: Aristocratic Kinship and Domestic Relations in Eighteenth-Century England* (New York: Academic Press, 1978); Elisabeth Badinter, *Émilie, Émilie: L'Ambition féminine au XVIIIème siècle* (Paris: Flammarion, 1983); Jacques Donzelot, *The Policing of Families*, trans. Robert Hurley (New York: Pantheon, 1979); Cissie Fairchild, "Women and Family," in *French Women in the Age of Enlightenment*, ed. Samia I. Spencer (Bloomington, IN: Indiana University Press, 1984), 97–110. See also Elizabeth Fox-Genovese and Eugene D. Genovese, *Fruits of Merchant Capital: Slavery and Bourgeois Property in the Rise and Expansion of Capitalism* (New York: Oxford University Press, 1983), ch. 11 "The Ideological Bases of Domestic Economy: The Representation of Women and the Family in the Age of Expansion."

Notes

4. Initially Talcott Parsons and his students pioneered in applying Weberian theory to family history. See, for example, Neil Smelser, *Social Change in the Industrial Revolution: An Application of Theory to the British Cotton Industry* (London: University of Chicago Press, 1959). Many subsequent histories of family life, including some excellent ones, have adapted a functional perspective to their own purposes. See, for example, David Levine, *Family Formation in an Age of Nascent Capitalism* (New York: Academic Press, 1977); David Levine, ed., *Proletarianization and Family History* (Orlando, FL: Academic Press, 1984); Hans Medick, "The Proto-Industrial Family Economy: The Structural Function of Household and Family during the Transition from Peasant Society to Industrial Capitalism," *Social History* 1, no. 3 (October 1976): 291–315; Michael Anderson, "Family, Household, and Industrial Revolution," in *The American Family in Social-Historical Perspective*, ed. Michael Gordon, 1st ed. (New York: St. Martin's, 1973); Michael Anderson, *Family Structure in Nineteenth-Century Lancashire* (Cambridge: Cambridge University Press, 1971); Michael Anderson, Frank Bechhofer, and Jonathan Gershuny, eds. *The Social and Political Economy of the Household* (Oxford: Oxford University Press, 1994); Peter Laslett, *Family and Household in Past Time* (Cambridge: Cambridge University Press, 1972). For a general sampling, see *The American Family in Social-Historical Perspective*, ed. Michael Gordon, 2nd. ed. (New York: St. Martin's, 1978) and 3rd. ed. (New York: St. Martin's, 1983). For a more explicit anthropological perspective, see, for example, Jack Goody, *Production and Reproduction* (Cambridge: Cambridge University Press, 1976); Nancie L. Gonzalez, *Black Carib Household Structure: A Study of Migration and Modernization* (Seattle: University of Washington Press, 1969). And, for a critique of functionalism, Christopher Lasch, *Haven in a Heartless World* (New York: Basic Books, 1977).

5. Good examples of this attitude may be found in Louise A. Tilly and Joan W. Scott, *Women, Work, and Family* (New York: Holt, Rinehart & Winston, 1978) and Darret B. Rutman and Anita H. Rutman, *A Place in Time: Middlesex County, Virginia, 1650–1750*, 2 vols. (New York: Norton, 1984).

6. The intrinsic value of marriage and family embodied in the changing forms of both emerges from a wide variety of studies. See, for example, Charles Rosenberg, ed. *The Family in History* (Philadelphia: University of Pennsylvania Press, 1975); Jack Goody, Joan Thirsk, and E. P. Thompson, eds., *Family and Inheritance: Rural Society in Western Europe, 1200–1800* (Cambridge: Cambridge University Press, 1976); Georges Duby, *i.e chevalier, la femme et le prêtre: le mariage dans la France féodale* (Paris: Hachette, 1981); Frances and Joseph Gies, *Marriage and the Family in the Middle Ages* (New York: Harper & Row, 1987); Barbara A. Hanawalt, *The Ties That Bound: Peasant Families in Medieval England* (New York: Oxford University Press, 1986); David Herlihy, *Medieval Households* (Cambridge, MA: Harvard University Press, 1985); Ernest Bertin, *Les Marriages dans l'ancienne société française* (Genève: Slatkin, 1975; orig. ed., 1879); Cristiane Klapisch-Zuber, *Women, Family, and Ritual in Renaissance Italy*, trans. Lydia G. Cochrane (Chicago: University of Chicago Press, 1985); Suzanne Fonay Wemple, *Women in Frankish Society: Marriage and the Cloister, 500–900* (Philadelphia: University of Pennsylvania Press, 1981); Herbert G. Gutman, *The Black Family in Slavery and Freedom, 1750–1925* (New York: Pantheon, 1976); J. Hajnal, "European Marriage Patterns in Perspective," in *Population in History: Essays in Historical Demography*, D. V. Glass and D. E. C. Eversley, eds. (London: E. Arnold, 1965); Paul Ourliac and J. de Malafosse, *Le Droit familial*, vol. 3 of *Histoire de droit privé* (Paris: Presses universitaires, 1968); Martine Segalen, *Mari et femme dans la société paysanne* (Paris: Flammarion, 1980); Jean-Louis Flandrin, *Families in Former Times*, trans. Richard Southern (Cambridge: Cambridge University Press, 1979).

7. For a more extended discussion, see Elizabeth Fox-Genovese, *Within the Plantation Household: Black and White Women of the Old South* (Chapel Hill, NC: University of North Carolina Press, 1988). See also Eugene D. Genovese, *Roll, Jordan, Roll: The World the Slaves Made* (New York: Pantheon, 1975); Gutman, *Black Family*; James Hugo Johnston, *Race Relations in Virginia and Miscegenation in the South, 1766–1860* (Amherst, MA: University of Massachusetts Press, 1970).

8. Robin Fox, *Kinship and Marriage: An Anthropological Perspective* (Harmmondsworth, UK: Penguin, 1974).

9. For a fuller discussion of the issues, especially the relation of individualism to family cohesion, see Elizabeth Fox-Genovese, *Feminism without Illusions: A Critique of Individualism* (Chapel Hill, NC: University of North Carolina Press, 1991).

10. For a fuller discussion, see James Gustafson, *Ethics From a Theocentric Perspective,* 2 vols. (Chicago: University of Chicago Press, 1984), 2: 153–84. See also Duby, *Le chevalier, la femme et le prêtre*; Steven Ozemont, *When Fathers Ruled: Family Life in Reformation Europe* (Cambridge, MA: Harvard University Press, 1983).

11. William N. Eskridge Jr., *The Case for Same-Sex Marriage: From Sexual Liberty to Civilized Commitment* (New York: Free Press, 1996); Sanford M. Dornbusch and Myra H. Strober, *Feminism, Children, and the New Families* (New York: Guilford Press, 1988); Sharon Elizabeth Rush, "Breaking With Tradition: Surrogacy and Gay Fathers," in *Kindred Matters: Rethinking the Philosophy of the Family,* ed. Diana Tietjens Meyers, Kenneth Kipnis, and Cornelius F. Murphy Jr. (Ithaca, NY: Cornell University Press, 1993), 102–142. For the opposing position, see, for example, Maggie Gallagher, *The Abolition of Marriage: How We Lost the Right to a Lasting Love* (New York: Regnery Publishing, 1996) and David Popenoe, *Life without Father: Compelling New Evidence that Fatherhood and Marriage Are Indispensable for the Good of Children and Society* (New York: Free Press, 1996).

12. See, for example, Carole Pateman, *The Sexual Contract* (Stanford, CA: Stanford University Press, 1988); Rosalind Coward, *Patriarchal Precedents: Sexuality and Social Relations* (London: Routledge & Kegan Paul, 1983); Ellen Willis, *No More Nice Girls: Countercultural Essays* (Hanover, NH: Wesleyan University Press, 1992); Adrienne Rich, "Compulsory Heterosexuality and the Lesbian Experience," *Signs: Journal of Women in Culture and Society* 4 (1980).

13. Sir Robert Filmer, *Patriarchia and Other Writings,* ed. Peter Laslett (Oxford: Basil Blackwell, 1949). See also Fox-Genovese, *Feminism without Illusions* and "Property and Patriarchy

in Early Bourgeois Political Culture," *Radical History Review* 4, nos. 2 & 3 (Spring/Summer 1977): 35–59. See also Gordon Schochet, *Patriarchalism in Political Thought: The Authoritarian Family and Political Speculation and Attitudes Especially in Seventeenth-Century England* (New York: Basic Books, 1975).

14. Suzanne Dixon, *The Roman Family* (Baltimore: Johns Hopkins University Press, 1992); Judith P. Hallett, *Fathers and Daughters in Roman Society: Women and the Elite Family* (Princeton, NJ: Princeton University Press, 1984); Louis de Loménie, Les Mirabeau: Nouvelles études sur la société française au XVIIIè siècle 5 vols. (Paris, 1879–1891).

15. William Blackstone, *Commentaries on the Laws of England*, 4 vols. (Chicago: University of Chicago Press, 1979; orig. ed., 1765–1769). See also Margaret J. M. Ezell, *The Patriarch's Wife: Literary Evidence and the History of the Family* (Chapel Hill, NC: University of North Carolina Press, 1987).

16. J. E. Neale, *Queen Elizabeth I* (New York: Doubleday-Anchor Books, 1957).

17. See, for example, Carroll Smith Rosenberg, *Disorderly Conduct: Visions of Gender in Victorian America* (New York: Alfred Knopf, 1985); Ellen Carol DuBois, *Feminism and Suffrage: The Emergence of an Independent Women's Movement in America, 1848–1869* (Ithaca, NY: Cornell University Press, 1978); Mary Roth Walsh, *Doctors Wanted: No Women Need Apply: Sexual Barriers in the Medical Profession, 1835–1975* (New Haven, CT: Yale University Press, 1977); Joan D. Hedrick, *Harriet Beecher Stowe* (New York: Oxford University Press, 1994); Brian Harrison, *Separate Spheres: The Opposition to Women's Suffrage in Britain* (New York: Holmes & Meier, 1978); Martha Vicinus, *Independent Women: Work and Community for Single Women, 1850–1920* (Chicago: University of Chicago Press, 1985); Mary Lyndon Shanley, *Feminism, Marriage, and the Law in Victorian England, 1850–1895* (Princeton, NJ: Princeton University Press, 1989); Steven C. Hause with Anne R. Kenney, *Women's Suffrage and Social Politics in the French Third Republic* (Princeton, NJ: Princeton University Press, 1984).

18. Gerda Lerner, *The Creation of Patriarchy* (New York: Oxford University Press, 1986) and Elizabeth Fox-Genovese's review of it in *Journal of the American Academy of Religion* 55, no. 3 (Fall 1987): 608–12.

19. Olwen Hufton, *The Prospect Before Her: A History of Women in Western Europe*, vol. 1, 1500–1800 (New York: Alfred A. Knopf, 1996), esp., 137–76. "On Being a Wife." See also, for example, M. Mitterauer and R. Sieder, *The European Family: From Patriarchy to Partnership from the Middle Ages to the Present* (Oxford: Oxford University Press, 1982); J. Goody, *The Development of the Family and Marriage in Europe* (Cambridge: Cambridge University Press, 1983); Elizabeth Fox-Genovese, "Women and Work," in *French Women and the Age of Enlightenment*, ed. Samia I. Spencer (Bloomington, IN: Indiana University Press, 1984), 111–127; François Lebrun, *La Vie conjugale sous l'ancien régime* (Paris: Armand Colin, 1975); Yves Castan, *Honnêteté et relations sociales en Languedoc (1750–1780)* (Paris: Plon, 1974); Segalen, *Mari et Femme*; Flandrin, *Families in Former Times*.

20. Hufton, *Prospect Before Her*; Olwen Hufton, *The Poor in Eighteenth-Century France* (Oxford: Oxford University Press, 1974); E. A. Wrigley and R. S. Schofield, *The Population History of England 1541–1871* (London: Edward Arnold, 1981); William Goode, *World Revolution and Family Patterns* (New York: Free Press of Glencoe, 1963).

21. Robert P. George and Gerard V. Bradley, "Marriage and the Liberal Imagination," *The Georgetown Law Journal* 84, no. 2 (Dec. 1995): 301–320. See also Robert P. George, "Natural Law and Positive Law," in *The Autonomy of Law*, ed. Robert P. George (Oxford: Clarendon Press, 1996), 321–34 and John Finnis, *Natural Law and Natural Rights* (Oxford: Clarendon Press, 1980).

22. Friederick Engels, *The Origin of the Family, Private Property and the State* (New York: International Publishers, 1972); Karen Sacks, *Mothers and Wives: The Past and Future of Sexual Equality* (Westport, CT: Greenwood Press, 1979).

23. For a fuller discussion of the significance, see Elizabeth Fox-Genovese, *"Feminism Is Not the Story of My Life': How Today's*

Feminist Elite Has Lost Touch with the Real Concerns of Women (New York: Doubleday, 1996) and on some of the implications of the recent sea change, see Richard A. Posner, *Sex and Reason* (Cambridge, MA: Harvard University Press, 1992), and reviews of Posner by Robert P. George, "Can Sex Be Reasonable," *Columbia Law Review* 93, no. 3 (April 1993): 783–94, and Elizabeth Fox-Genovese, "Beyond Transgression: Toward a Free Market in Morals," *Yale Journal of Law and the Humanities* 5, no. 1 (Winter 1993): 243–64.

24. John Locke, *Two Treatises of Government*, ed. Peter Laslett (Cambridge: Cambridge University Press, 1960 and John Locke, *An Essay Concerning Human Understanding*, 2 vols., ed. Alexander Campbell Fraser (New York: Dover, 1959). See also Elizabeth Fox-Genovese, "Property and Patriarchy in Early Bourgeois Political Culture," *Radical History Review* 4, nos. 2 and 3 (Spring/Summer 1977): 36–59.

25. Notwithstanding some persisting disagreements about timing and effect on the lives of the mass of the population, this view has attained general acceptance, and versions of it pervade most of the vast literature on family and women's history, some of which is cited above.

26. For an elaboration, see Fox-Genovese, *"Feminism Is Not the Story of My Life."*

27. Mary Jo Bane, *Here to Stay: American Families in the Twentieth Century* (New York: Basic Books, 1976).

Chapter 6: The Legal Status of Families as Institutions

1. William Blackstone, "Of the Rights of Persons," in vol. 1, *Commentaries of the Laws of England* (Chicago: University of Chicago Press, 1979 [1765]), 430.

2. E.g., Angelina Grimkê, "Letters to Catherine Beecher, Letter XII," in *The Feminist Papers: From Adam to de Beauvoir*, Alice S. Rossi, ed. (New York: Columbia University Press, 1973), 320–22. For the general use of the metaphor, see Blanche Glassman Hersh, *The Slavery of Sex: Feminist-Abolitionists in America* (Urbana, IL: University of Illinois Press, 1978).

3. For the general use of the metaphor, see Elizabeth Fox-Geno-vese, *Within the Plantation Household: Black and White Women of the Old South* (Chapel Hill, NC: University of North Caro-lina Press, 1988), 101.

4. John Locke, "The Second Treatise of Government," in *Two Treatises of Government*, ed. Peter Laslett (Cambridge: Cam-bridge University Press, 1960), §82.

5. Norma Basch, *In the Eyes of the Law: Women, Marriage, and Property in Nineteenth-Century New York* (Ithaca, NY: Cornell University Press, 1982).

6. For an insightful discussion positing that individual rights for children are "wrong rights," see Elizabeth Wolgast, *The Gram-mar of Justice* (Ithaca, NY: Cornell University Press, 1987), 28–38.

7. On the law of slavery, see Mark V. Tushnet, *The American Law of Slavery, 1810–1860: Considerations of Humanity and Interest* (Princeton, NJ: Princeton University Press, 1981) and Eugene D. Genovese, *Roll, Jordan, Roll: The World the Slaves Made* (New York: Pantheon, 1974).

8. See Wolgast, *The Grammar of Justice*, 28–38.

Chapter 7: Historical Perspectives on the Human Person

1. Quoted in *Presbyterians Pro-Life News* (Fall 2000): 3.

Index

Index

About the Author and Editor

Elizabeth Fox-Genovese (1941–2007) was the Eléonore Raoul Professor of the Humanities and Professor of History at Emory University, where she was also the founding director of the Institute for Women's Studies. She received the National Humanities Medal from President Bush in 2003, was a member of the Governing Council of the National Endowment for the Humanities, and was a recipient of the Cardinal Wright Award from the Fellowship of Catholic Scholars. Her books include *Within the Plantation Household: Black and White Women of the Old South*; *Feminism without Illusions: A Critique of Individualism*; and *The Mind of the Master Class: History and Faith in the Southern Slaveholders' Worldview* (coauthored with Eugene D. Genovese).

Sheila O'Connor-Ambrose, who holds a Ph.D. in women's studies from Emory University, is an independent scholar whose main academic interests include women writers, feminist theory, and the role of Catholicism in contemporary culture. She is a fellow of The Alexander Hamilton Institute for the Study of Western Civilization in Clinton, New York.